Flowers and Colour
IN WINTER

FLOWERS AND COLOUR
IN WINTER

PATRICK M. SYNGE
VMH

Country & Gardeners Book Society

READERS UNION GROUP

Flowers in Winter
by Patrick M Synge
originally published by
LINDSAY DRUMMOND LTD,
1948

This edition, enlarged and revised
as *Flowers and Colour in Winter*,
published 1974 by
Readers Union
by arrangement with
Michael Joseph Limited

ISBN 0 7181 1213 X

Set and printed in Great Britain
by Tonbridge Printers Ltd,
Peach Hall Works, Tonbridge, Kent
in Baskerville eleven on thirteen point
and bound by
James Burn at Esher, Surrey

Contents

THE WINTER GARDEN   11

BULBS AND TUBERS   24
Anemones and Pulsatillas; Crocuses; Cyclamen; Iris;
Miniature and early Daffodils; Snowdrops and Snowflakes; Tulips. A miscellany of Bulbs and Tubers:
Winter Aconites, Scillas, Chionodoxas, Muscaris, Colchicums, Tecophilaeas, Puschkinias, Hyacinthus, Erythroniums and Fritillaries

HERBS   59
Celandines, Hepaticas, Periwinkles and Violets; Helle-
bores; Primulas; Pulmonarias and Lithospermums;
Saxifrages

TREES AND SHRUBS   73
Camellias; Cherries, Almonds, Peaches, Apricots and
Plums; Daphnes; Hamamelis; Heathers; Magnolias;
Mahonias; Rhododendrons; Viburnums; Willows

SOME OTHER GOOD WINTER PLANTS   111
Abeliophyllum; Acacias; Adonis; Alnus; Arbutus; Ber-
genias; Chaenomeles; Chimonanthus; Clematis; Cornus;
Corylopsis; Fatsia and Fatshedera; Forsythias; Garrya;
Hebe; Honeysuckles; Osmanthus; Parrotia; Pieris;
Ribes; Sarcococcas; Schizostylis; Sternbergia; Sycopsis

BERRIES AND FRUITS IN WINTER   127

COLOURED BARK IN THE WINTER GARDEN   136

FORM AND FOLIAGE IN THE WINTER GARDEN   142

THE COOL GREENHOUSE IN WINTER   148

INDEX   155

Illustrations

COLOUR PLATES

1 The stylosa iris. *I unguicularis*, by many considered
the finest winter-flowering plant   80
Hamamelis mollis 'Pallida' which usually flowers in
January   80
2 *Magnolia campbellii*. Some consider this the most
magnificent of all flowering trees   81
3 *Cyclamen coum* in January or early February.   96
Snowdrops at Kew   96
Eranthis x *tubergenii*, a hybrid and the finest winter
aconite   96
Erythronium 'White Beauty'   96
4 *Primula whitei*, a lovely Petiolarid primula   97
Camellia x *williamsii* 'Donation', one of the most
free-flowering camellias   97
Skimmia japonica whose berries last throughout the
winter   97
Cornus stolonifera 'Flaviramea' and *C. alba* 'Sibirica'   97

BLACK AND WHITE PLATES

1 The Winter Jasmine, *Jasminum nudiflorum*   16
The Stylosa iris, *Iris unguicularis* 'Mary Barnard'   16
2 *Tibouchina semidecandra*   17
Rhododendron lindleyi   17
3 *Anemone blanda*. The deep blue variety *atrocoerulea*   32
Anemone nemorosa 'Allenii'   32
4 *Pulsatilla vernalis*   33
Crocus chrysanthus 'E.A. Bowles', still one of the finest
of the deep yellow varieties   33
5 Crocuses at Kew   40
Iris histrioides major in early March   40

6   *Narcissus cantabricus* var. *petunioides*, a very early white variety   40

Narcissus asturiensis   40

7   *Galanthus* 'Straffan' and *Crocus tomasinianus*   40

Leucojum vernum   40

Tulipa kaufmanniana   40

8   *Eranthis hyemalis*, the common winter aconite   41

Scilla bifolia   41

Chionodoxa luciliae   41

9   *Erythronium citrinum*   48

Tecophilaea cyanocrocus   48

Fritillaria acmopetala   48

10   *Helleborus niger*, the Christmas rose   48

Helleborus atrorubens   48

11   *Primula edgeworthii*   48

Primula 'Wanda'   48

Primula clarkei   48

12   *Saxifraga oppositifolia* 'Splendens'   48

Saxifraga 'Faldonside'   48

Viola septentrionalis   48

13   *Camellia reticulata* 'Noble Pearl' one of the finest Chinese forms   48

14   The best almond, *Prunus* 'Pollardii'   48

15   *Prunus subhirtella autumnalis* 'Rosea'   48

Prunus x *blireana*, an early hybrid between *Prunus* 'Pissardi' and an apricot   48

16   *Daphne mezereum*, a fine specimen of the white form   48

Daphne blagayana   48

17   *Prunus triloba*   48

Erica carnea, the winter flowering heath   48

18   *Hamamelis mollis*, the witch hazel   49

19   *Magnolia* x *soulangiana*, an old specimen   64

20   *Magnolia stellata* at Kew   65

Magnolia campbellii subsp. *mollicomata*, a lovely flower in a famous Cornish garden   65

21   *Mahonia* 'Charity'   112

22   *Rhododendron* 'Seta'   113

23 *Rhododendron* 'Tessa Roza', a very early flowering
    hybrid   128
    Rhododendron x *praecox*   128
24 *Viburnum* x *bodnantense* 'Deben'   128
    Viburnum carlesii, a fine specimen   128
25 *Salix aegyptiaca*   128
26 Fluffy willow catkins decorate the late winter
    landscape   128
27 *Abeliophyllum distichum*   128
    Arbutus unedo   128
28 *Bergenia* 'Ballawley'   **128**
    Chaenomeles japonica   128
29 *Cornus mas*   128
30 *Fatsia japonica*   128
31 *Forsythia* x *intermedia* 'Spectabilis'   128
    Pieris japonica   128
32 *Garrya elliptica*   128
33 *Ribes sanguineum*   128
34 *Celastrus orbiculatus*, a most spectacular climber   129
35 *Cotoneaster conspicuus* var. *decorus*, one of the
    brightest red late autumn fruiting shrubs   136
36 *Acer griseum* shows its peeling mahogany bark   136
    Arbutus x *andrachnoides*   136
37 *Betula jacquemontii*, one of the finest white trunked
    birches   136
    Rubus cockburnianus which used to be called *R.
    giraldianus*   136
38 *Picea brewerana*   137
39 The grey needled form of *Pinus montezumae* from
    Mexico   144
40 *Jasminum polyanthum*   145
    Rhododendron 'White Wings'   145

The Winter Garden

I have always found that winter flowers give me special and peculiar pleasure. Even the smallest winter flowers seem desirable and exciting, for there is so little else then; as summer flowers many of them would not hold their place among the more luxuriant and sumptuous beauties, and would be quickly rooted out.

This little book does not claim to be a complete record of all plants that may flower during the winter in England. Rather is it a selection of well tried subjects which can be confidently recommended. Few of the plants mentioned are very new or little known, yet in how few gardens do we meet more than two or three of them, perhaps the stylosa iris and the winter jasmine, perhaps an occasional hellebore. Few of them again are expensive, in fact the majority will cost under the pound and can be obtained without difficulty through any big nurseryman. Though perhaps less satisfying and less exciting than propagating at home, the owner of a small garden who has little spare time and who has only space for a very few plants of each will find this the best means of building up a collection of winter flowers.

Again, so variable is our climate that it is impossible to define an average winter. I have compromised by including plants which will flower in the home counties, such as Surrey or Sussex, between the beginning of November and the end of March. Their exact date of flowering will vary enormously from year to year and will partly depend on those mild periods which we often have to break the cold spell, and which will bring on our flowers so quickly that in a week or a fortnight the garden will be transformed. The flowers are always there awaiting just that little extra bit of warmth. In the warmer, damper parts of the country, such as Devon and Cornwall and the western coast of Scotland, many more plants can be grown and will flower freely during the winter. In the home and more northern counties it is always a bit of a gamble. A brief mild spell may bring the buds to the opening state when they are vulnerable and they may be carried off in a night. However, it is a gamble which can be repeated from year to year and there are very few years in which one loses all along the line. In fact the successes are encouragingly frequent once the hazard is made. November and December are, perhaps, the leanest months, but in other ways, in replanting and planning, they are such busy months that the lack of flowers is hardly noticed. Also there are generally some hangovers from October, lingering chrysanthemums, maybe a few bulbs such as *Amaryllis belladonna*, *Nerine bowdenii* or *Schizostylis coccinea*. Although primarily autumnal, some of the brilliance of autumn colouring in maples and rhus may hang on into November, but these are not really a true part of the garden of winter flowers. Berries and the decoration of trees with fine bark and exciting and ornamental foliage are more worthy of consideration in this aspect, although they are not technically flowers, but so important are they in planning that chapters about them have been added. It is in winter that we notice most the form of trees and shrubs: the white trunks and graceful feathery twigs of the silver birch, light against a dark sky, the formal pyramid of a cypress, towering and quivering like a cathedral spire towards the heavens or standing firm and round as a Celtic tower, the polished chestnut coloured trunk of *Acer griseum* or *Prunus serrula* like a piece of old mahogany. Even the forms of *Prunus serrulata*, to which most of our flowering cherries belong, have fine bark. I knew one old gentleman who, in the winter, kept a duster by these trees and gave the trunks a polish every day on his morning walk, flaking away the old papery bark.

The exploration of China and Tibet has extended the number of fine winter-flowering plants; still, the two best of all, which should be in every garden, have been grown in this country for over a hundred years. I refer to *Jasminum nudiflorum* and *Iris unguicularis*, more generally called *Iris stylosa*.

The Winter Jasmine was introduced from China by Robert

Fortune in the early part of the nineteenth century. He was sent out by the Council of the Royal Horticultural Society to collect plants there, and brought back a very large number of fine things.

Every year about November the long yellow buds become flushed with red on the bare green branches and open as five-pointed yellow stars. They are delicate, clean flowers, not very large but strong in colour, like a savoury rather than a sumptuous sweet. It is such a familiar favourite with all gardeners in this country that it is hard to find anything new to tell you about it. It is generally grown against a wall, south, west, east, and even north for a succession of flower. It will continue from November till March, and the more its bare twigs are cut for the house, the better the plant seems to flower next year. So do not hesitate. Prune while it is in flower and enjoy the prunings; they are particularly lovely in a dark chocolate-brown vase. Don't overcrowd them, but try and form a pattern picture, almost a Japanese decoration, so that the shadow gives you yet another picture on the wall, changing from every angle. If the vase could be poised so that it could swing round and round, then you could have a composition as satisfying as many of those fascinating toys of turning wire sometimes seen in art galleries interested in experimental work.

Miss Jekyll once suggested growing the Winter Jasmine cascading over a great rock, and for those lucky few who have great rocks in their gardens or can cascade climbers from one terrace to another, this method should be ideal. The winter jasmine can also be grown away from walls, and with the aid of sticks and hard pruning be made into a shapely mass extruding young shoots all round like a hedgehog. In this country I have always found that it was of cast-iron hardiness, although I have read that in American gardens it is not always a success and they sometimes resent the panegyrics which they find of it in English gardening books.

Jasminum nudiflorum has no soft sweet scent like the common jasmine. It is almost scentless, although strong scent is a common characteristic of winter flowers. There are few sweeter-smelling plants than *Chimonanthus praecox, Daphne mezereum* or *Viburnum farreri.*

Even larger in flower is *Jasminum mesnyi,* still more commonly known as *J. primulinum,* although this plant is successful outside only in the warmer counties. It is, however, an excellent plant for the cool greenhouse or conservatory, and is evergreen. It requires lots of room and looks best cascading in yellow streams from a high roof. In such a way I first saw it in the corridor of the greenhouses in the Cambridge Botanic Garden. The flowers are semi-double, about twice the diameter of those of *J. nudiflorum* and the same strong clear yellow, faintly pencilled with orange towards the centre. They are borne on short side shoots off the young growth.

Iris unguicularis is a native of Algeria and the eastern Mediterranean, warm sunny lands where it grows in open woodland. Yet it is one of the hardiest of our winter-flowering plants and the flowers are some of the most delicate and beautiful of all irises. They are a soft mauve in colour, the petals clear and translucent, slightly sparkling in the sunlight. The falls have a brilliant orange band running from the base to the centre of the petal, while around this is a white zone delicately pencilled with the mauve which is the main colour of the flower. The standards are mauve, slightly flecked with purplish-crimson towards the base.

I wonder how many growers of the plant have noticed that colouring, yet to my mind the markings of the falls and the base of the standards are some of its chief beauties. The whole flower has a graceful fairy-like charm; yet it is not small, rather the opposite, for it is a good four inches across. It is also distinguished from all other irises by the extremely long perianth tube, sometimes as long as nine inches, and by the curious processes which cover the branches of the style (those three pale forked pieces standing upright and away from the centre of the flower). Dykes, in his great work on irises, states that these are little transparent spheres poised on the top of equally transparent blunt cones. Inside the sphere there is a mass of golden grains, fine like dust, and it is these grains which give the style the curious appearance of being dusted with pale golden dust. Nowhere else in the genus iris is this phenomenon found.

Although *Iris unguicularis* has its chief home in Algeria, it is also found in many other parts of the Mediterranean: Greece, the islands of the Greek Archipelago, Crete, Asia Minor and northern Syria. There is also a form found on the shores of the Black Sea, which has been called var. *lazica*. It has much wider green leaves than the type and they stand more erect. The flower is dark purplish-blue, the petals wider, and the venation is more conspicuous than in the Algerian plant. The forms from Greece have not been given varietal names. They generally have smaller flowers than the Algerian forms and begin to flower much later, in March instead of in November. There are several garden varieties. Two of the best of these are 'Walter Butt', which has very pale lavender-blue almost jade-like petals, and 'Mary Barnard', which has slightly smaller flowers of a very rich violet and is well marked with gold. The late Bertram Anderson, an unusually knowledgeable gardener, recorded that it was the most free-flowering variety that he had. These are now available from some specialist nurserymen.

A most beautiful deep blue form, almost sapphire-blue in colour, was shown in 1946 at one of the Royal Horticultural Society's spring shows under the name of 'Ellis's Var', having been brought from a Riviera garden and established in Sussex. It was the finest blue form that I have yet seen. On the Riviera it was known as 'La Belle Pamela'! There are several good ivory-white forms also in cultivation but unfortunately they are rare. A mauve form with a narrow white edge to the petal has been named 'Marginata'. The variety from Crete, var. *cretensis*, is very distinct and has sometimes been regarded as a separate species. The leaves are the narrowest in the species and the flowers are pinkish-purple with strong gold markings. Unfortunately, though, it is so shy to bloom in cultivation that most of us will have to go to Crete in April to see it in flower, a journey well worth while for then Crete is literally an island of flowers. All the stylosas are excellent for picking for the house. The buds should be given a slight twist and a sharp pull and they will then come away with the long tube which serves them as stem.

Following the general custom, we have neither moved our clumps nor have we given them any manure, and they have rewarded us with many flowers though more in our old Surrey garden than in our more recent Sussex one where the soil is heavier. However, friends to whom we have given pieces off some of our bigger clumps, have often had good flowers off them the first year after moving and sometimes, alas, have even had them slightly earlier than ourselves. E. B. Anderson suggested that August was the best month to split up and divide clumps.

There is a very strong and prevalent theory that the *Iris unguicularis* should never be given any manure and should be planted for best results at the edge of a gravel path. Certainly it does better in light and gravelly positions than in heavy clay soil. But I find that Dykes himself, in his great monograph 'The Genus Iris', advocates the encouragement of spring and early summer growth with moisture and even weak liquid manure. No more water than the heavens deliver should be given after June, when the plant should be allowed to roast as much as possible. It is still a debatable point whether it is advisable to cut back the long foliage in summer so as to allow more sun to get to the rhizomes. I have never found that it mattered very much.

The small bulbous irises also brighten the winter months, *I. reticulata*, *I. histrioides* and *I. danfordiae*. I particularly like the two first species. *Iris reticulata* is a delicate, graceful thing in rich purple apparel with strong orange markings, yet in spite of all their apparent frailty and delicateness the flowers stand up magnificently to frosts and winter weather. Towards the end of January the fat buds appear and in February and early March they are often in flower. There are now many good forms and hybrids, discussed in the section on Iris.

The early crocus species and the miniature daffodils are also

(*Left*) The Winter Jasmine, *Jasminum nudiflorum*, one of the really indispensable plants for winter flowers. (J. E. Downward)

(*Right*) The Stylosa iris, *Iris unguicularis* 'Mary Barnard', a particularly fine deep mauve form. (J. E. Downward)

(*Above*) *Tibouchina semidecandra*, a wonderful rich purple flower for the cool greenhouse, flowering often from October till January. (H. Smith)

(*Below*) *Rhododendron lindleyi*, one of the finest tender rhododendrons for a cool greenhouse. This is the clone 'Dame Edith Sitwell' raised by Mr Geoffrey Gorer of Haywards Heath. (J. E. Downward)

well worth a place, especially if a little temporary protection can be given them from heavy rain and also from pecking birds, who seem to love especially the choicest crocus. The little *Crocus olivieri* has flowers as strong in orange as a marigold, while the fine variations of *Crocus chrysanthus* recall the brilliant colourings of the birds after which many of them are so aptly named. Nor should we forget the brilliant orange Cloth of Gold so attractively flecked and streaked with rich mahogany, *Crocus susianus*, while the great orange splashes of the common Dutch yellow crocus at the base of a tree, opening in the early sun, are one of the first signs of spring that we look for each year.

The arrangement of winter-flowering plants requires great care. If they are merely dotted among the other shrubs of the garden much of their effect will be lost. On the other hand many of them present no display from a distance. Their attraction lies in the delicate formation of the flower often accompanied by strong and very sweet scent. Scent is one of the predominant and most valuable characteristics of winter-flowering plants and it is this characteristic which makes them so valuable for picking for the house. However, to grow winter-flowering plants merely in rows across the kitchen garden as flowers for cutting is almost a confession that one never visits the garden in winter. Also some of the sweetest smelling plants such as daphnes will not tolerate excessive or regular cutting. If there is sufficient space available a small winter garden will surely provide a good return. It should be sheltered from east and north winds and should face either south or south-west. Some plants will fare better sheltered slightly from the early morning sun so that their buds may have time to thaw out before the sun reaches them after a cold night. Again, the winter garden should not be too far distant from the house, so that one can pop out to it in sunny spells. If a bay or a corner against the wall of the house is available it would probably prove an excellent site, especially if the chimney of a boiler or commonly used fireplace should ascend at the back of it. In that case one's stylosas will be a month or so earlier than one's neighbours', and one can also attempt such things as the mimosa *Acacia dealbata* which in such a situation as that at Wisley once overtopped the house, flowering every year, and even after being cut to the ground in a particularly severe winter sprang up again and was almost up to the eaves in two years' time – only to be killed later by a sudden very severe frost in a spell of mild weather. If successful the grey-blue trunk and finely divided foliage of this species will be a pleasure throughout the year.

If it is not possible to back the winter garden with the wall of a house or an old brick wall it would be well to screen it from the north and east by a belt of conifers. At any rate conifers should play a part in it and their rich greens and formal shapes should be used to contrast and display the winter flowers, the majority of which are light in tone. No one has yet succeeded in making any form out of a plant such as *Viburnum farreri* which is essentially formless and needs the juxtaposition of more formal plants. Many of the winter-flowering plants are best placed in groups for effect. This particularly applies to daphnes, which are easily raised from seed. If planted singly they tend to appear very lank and leggy and few seem to attain to a really fine bushy old age. If they do they scent the air around and form a bush, as thick as high, covered with flowers deep rose-pink or purple or white. In colour they are very variable and seedlings should be selected with care. Hamamelis and rhododendron will form an important part of the winter garden. A particularly successful combination is that of a group of the bright yellow *H. mollis* or even a single fine specimen flanked by a group of the purple-flowering *Rhododendron mucronulatum*. In a favourable season these two will flower together in January, often indeed as early as New Year's Day, and both will stand some frost inland. Then the creamy-white *Rhododendron moupinense* is well worth a sheltered place, but the large swelling buds and flowers are rather more susceptible to frost than those of *R. mucronulatum*. Another beautiful creamy flowering species is *R. leucaspis* and this is worth a very sheltered corner in the south but will only rarely be successful outside in the colder Midlands. However, this anticipates the section on rhododendrons.

If the winter garden is formed as part of a wild garden, wonderful pictures can be made by the skilful use of drifts of bulbs, snowdrops, dwarf daffodils and crocus, while hellebore and the rich purple primula 'Wanda' are a happy combination where the 'Wanda' will draw the eye from a distance so that one is irresistibly led to examine the hellebores. The flowers droop and it is worth lifting the flower heads in a close inspection.

Since many of the choicest flowering winter bulbs are dwarf, they are best enjoyed when planted either on a raised part of the rock garden or in some other way which brings them up nearly to waist level. In this respect the device of a bulb frame provides a successful raised winter garden in itself, and combines with some protection the quick drainage and capability for summer ripening that many of our winter-flowering bulbs demand, coming as they do from Asia Minor and the Mediterranean. It will be found that Chinese and North American plants are very much more tolerant of both winter and summer damp than are the Mediterranean and Persian species. Again, in a small space such a number of interesting plants can be grown, each one displayed naturally against little rocks or granite chips or even brick chips. All through the winter from January to April there should be something in flower in such a miniature garden, and it will be easy to see raised to waist level, while if there is a glass against the winter rains the blossoms will be undashed. The only trouble is keeping some of the plants in sufficient restraint so that they do not smother their neighbours. But again, bulbs flower well when growing through a carpet of dwarf shrubs, provided that these are really dwarf.

We made a small scree frame in my former garden in 1939 as an attempt to grow choicer alpines without constant labour, and many bulbs and other plants survived the six years of war there absolutely without attention. Against the front wall of a small lean-to greenhouse facing south, but in a position sheltered by the house from the early morning sun, we built out a wall three and a half feet high on the three remaining sides. Into the bottom of this we put a six-inch layer of bits of brick, stones, and even a few fragments of old and useless earthenware which had been lying round the garden for many years in disused corners. Above this we put a layer of upturned turves to hold the compost. This we mixed with care and as thoroughly as one would mix a fine cake. We used 2 parts finely crushed brick, 1 part washed coarse Cornish sand, 1 part Sorbex peat well damped and 1 part sterilised potting soil. This last item is rather richer food than is generally given to alpines, but combined with the good drainage it proved very successful and some of the Kabschia saxifrages grew together like a Persian rug with the same attractive irregularities and the same rich sparkling jewels.

The alpine house provides a wonderful display in the early spring, and after visiting such a model as the one at Wisley there are few who do not momentarily wish to do likewise, probably little realising the constant labour of maintaining a large collection of alpines in pans or the number of extra frames required to keep a constant display in the house. However, in a more modest way it is very well worth while to grow a few really fine large pans of early dwarf bulbs or alpines plunged in a frame, which can be brought into the house for flowering. Often a well-grown pan of miniature daffodils such as *N. cyclamineus*, or one of the hybrids such as 'Beryl' or 'W. P. Milner', will prove a more attractive centre-piece on the table than a bowl of rather larger flowering varieties and one can easily bring them into flower during February or March.

Again I regret the disappearance of the Georgian and Victorian winter garden. However, modern electric heating with thermostatic control has made more greenhouses possible, and for a house kept below a minimum of 45°F. in winter the cost is not prohibitive and some such houses have been built and stocked and they give better light than in the older Victorian conservatories or Georgian orangery. Of course, if one can approach such a house as an extension of one of the

rooms of the house it is doubly valuable in winter, and sometimes the same heating system can economically heat both
greenhouse and dwelling house. The finest house for such
plants that I know is the big one in the Savill Garden of
Windsor Great Park and this is open in late winter each year
when the flowers are at their best. This is tall enough to allow
growth of tree-like camellias and rhododendrons. Few of us
will be able to afford such a house, but from a much smaller
one we have derived enormous pleasure and many flowers.
It requires much less heat and labour to keep a house planted
out mainly with very early-flowering shrubs than it does to
keep a conservatory full of pot plants in flower and to renew
them as they go over. It is also much more natural, although
there is never enough space and it can easily tend to become
rather a jungle. Still, most shrubs can be pruned quite severely
or renewed with younger specimens. So I have added to this
edition a chapter on the cool greenhouse in winter.

The value of one big specimen of *Camellia reticulata* is so
great and so little heat is really required. A control set just
above freezing point would suffice and the electricity would
probably only need to operate on a small proportion of the
winter nights. Its drying effect would cause no harm, in fact
might well prove a benefit for such plants. Such fine mauve
flowering shrubs as *Tibouchina semidecandra* will flower in such a
house from September till February, after which they should
be cut hard back, almost right down to the ground to produce
young growths for next year. I know no other flowers so royal
in their purple, so rich and velvety as those of the *Tibouchina*.
They form large flat saucers often three or four inches in
diameter, while the stigmas project like a farmer's pronged
fork out of the centre of the flower. They are regal in every
respect, even the rich crinkly leaves, so characteristic of
Melastomaceous plants. The petals have a satin sheen which
makes them gleam as the light is reflected. In our small greenhouse we have grown the big annual white *Ipomoea bona-nox*
behind it, and since this latter seldom reaches flowering size
before the end of September or October, the two blend happily

together during this month and November. The great white flowers open at sunset and remain till the following midday.

Then the *Epacris* (heather-like shrubs from Australia) and the Cape heaths are fascinating winter-flowering plants in the cultivation of which our ancestors undoubtedly excelled us. In fact many have been lost in England today and should be reintroduced. A collection of the Cape heaths would be a speciality that would give much pleasure, and much information can be obtained about them from the old books such as Andrew's wonderful book on heaths which is full of magnificent colour plates. I feel also that a revival should be stimulated in the cultivation of pelargoniums. Hardly anywhere now does one see a named collection of pelargoniums, yet many of them will make an attractive display in winter both in flowers and leaf. I well remember a visit at Christmas to an old house in Devonshire which had a conservatory running along the whole of one side and the white-washed walls were covered with climbing pelargoniums in varying shades of pink, flowering in large clusters. No artificial heat was given them at all. We are inclined to forget that there used to be many more pelargoniums than the scarlet geranium 'Paul Crampel'. Very little water or attention is required during the winter, and probably the drier they are left the more resistant they will be to cold. To raise young plants for winter flowering the cuttings should be inserted in March or April and the flower buds nipped out until the beginning of September.

A walk round the temperate house at Kew or Wisley during the winter months shows how much can be grown which will flower when there is little outside. Often an old peach or vine house can be converted. In addition to the pelargoniums, heaths, *Tibouchina* and *Epacris* already mentioned, many of the tenderer rhododendrons of the *Maddenii* and *Edgeworthii* series such as *R. edgeworthii*, which has creamy-white fragrant flowers and puckered leaves, camellias and even almonds, peaches and forsythias will flower much earlier than outside and the flowers will be clean and protected against the weather.

For convenience this book is divided into sections of bulbs, of herbs, and of shrubs, but in the garden there should be no division. The three should grow together and help each other to build up winter pictures. Since many winter-flowering plants are soft in tone, those which are strong such as *Crocus chrysanthus*, *Primula* 'Wanda' or *Rhododendron mucronulatum* should be used to contrast with them and draw attention to them.

Finally, I hope this little book will encourage many more gardeners to gamble a little with winter-flowering plants. So often the odds will be in their favour and it is a gamble which can be repeated each year without any further stake. The field of winter-flowering plants is also one towards which the hybridist and plant selector might profitably turn his attention, as also the plant collector, though in its native habitat it will often be difficult to recognise the plant which will be a winter flowerer in England. Often the harder winter of northern America or China will restrain them from flowering till the spring thaws the ground.

Bulbs and Tubers

ANEMONES AND PULSATILLAS

The blue Windflower *Anemone blanda* seems like a patch of blue sky reflected in the ground in early March. Opening only with the sun, it is nevertheless very resistant to cold and frost. It is a very persistent plant. When I returned and considered the jungle that the War had left in my garden and the inevitable digging of the bed in which my anemones had been, I feared that they might have been lost as no tubers were apparent at the time. However, I soon saw them showing up, the bud delicately cupped under the leaf, and digging only served to spread the clumps still more widely.

No anemone has the deep, rich blue of a gentian or an anchusa, but it is a brilliant blue, nevertheless, in which white lightens the intensity, but hardly the brilliance. It is nearer a sky-blue than the gentian.

Anemone blanda is an inhabitant of the Greek mountains, and flowers early with us, in February and March. It is important to secure good forms to start colonies. The deepest blue is that variety called *atrocoerulea* which was sometimes known as *ingrami*. It is a wild plant of Greece and was the basis of the magnificent display at Highdown, Sir Frederick Stern's old garden near Worthing. He recorded that only six tubers were sent to him from Greece and now they have spread to many thousands, liking the warm soil and the chalk. In this form the stars have a small mixture of the wine-dark sea mixed with the sky-blue. The disc is golden in the centre of the rich blue petals. The flowers are star shaped but amply petalled, and are often several inches across. The finest pink forms are 'Charmer' and 'Radar', the latter being larger and darker in colour. 'Violetta' also has large flowers, a mauve-purple with white centre, while 'White Beauty' has the largest flowers of all, nearly twice the size of the normal form. Some may like to mingle all these together when they will seed to form a Persian carpet or tapestry effect, a coat of many colours. The variety *scythinica* has blue outside and white inside the petals but is much less vigorous. It comes from the windy moorlands near the top of the Pontus range north-east in Turkey.

Later in March comes the better known *Anemone appenina*. This is an even more variable plant, but the best blue forms are very desirable and the flowers stand up on slightly stouter stems than those of the Greek *A. blanda*. There is a white form and a pinkish form and, rather rare, a double white. I never feel, though, that this has the clear maenad-like grace of the single forms.

These anemones are essentially wild flowers brought by us into the garden – and not garden forms. If you want these, and they are very brilliant in colour, buy the poppy anemones, *A. coronaria*, such as the named single forms: 'Hollandia' which is frequently also called 'His Excellency' and is scarlet with white centre, 'Mr Fokker' a good blue, 'Sylphide' violet, or 'The Bride' white, or a good mixed strain such as De Caen or just Giant French. These are close to the wild ones you may find in Greece and the eastern Mediterranean islands though they rarely seem to grow mixed there. They are mainly plants of the lowland although I have seen mauve ones upon the Plain of Omalo in Crete at 3,000 feet. In Greece they flower in March or early April. There are fine stands of the scarlet ones around Athens. Some may prefer the semi-double and think that they last longer when cut. The best strain of these is still the St Brigid, while named single colours are called after unnamed dignitaries: 'The Admiral' violet-mauve, 'The Governor' scarlet or 'Lord Lieutenant' blue. The knobbly tubers of these and the St Bavo strain should be planted in a warm sunny place in September-October for late winter and early spring flowering or they can be grown from seed. In parts of Cornwall their cultivation has become an industry.

The grace and wildness of the blue forms is carried over into the glistening scarlet of *A. fulgens*, rather a mystery plant in origin but one that has spread widely in the south of France and also in the forms of the Great Peacock anemone *A. pavonina* from Greece and the eastern Mediterranean islands. The finest is the scarlet, either with a white eye or just with a little black centre, and this is one of the most dazzling flowers I know. That glorious strain of many colours the St Bavo hybrids, is close to the wild flowers, ranging to scarlet through many shades of pink and cream and white. I prefer them to the stiffer Poppy anemones and in some gardens such as Highdown they have naturalised themselves, spreading by seeding, flowering at about the same time as *A. blanda.*

Finally, our own wild wood *Anemone nemorosa* and its many colour forms make charming colonists, often spreading till they cover large areas, mingling with the primroses and flowering in late March and early April. The sight of these wild wood ones carpeting a beech wood is surely one of the loveliest our native flowers can offer. The finest of the forms is 'Allenii' which has a larger flower than the type, a pale rosy-lilac outside and soft lavender-blue inside. The deepest blue is probably 'Royal Blue' but this may be difficult to obtain, and there is also a lovely white, larger than the common wild form, called 'Vestal'.

About the origin and derivation of the name *Anemone*, not to mention the correct pronunciation which is of course tied to the derivation, there is still much doubt and controversy. The popular and accepted derivation is from the Greek word 'anemos', wind, and for this the wish is undoubtedly father to the thought, for it is most apt. Farrer, however, will not allow this and gives us instead a derivation on the authority of the Frenchman Tournefort, which he asserts is prior to Linnaeus's derivation. He derives the word from the Syrian cry 'Na-ma'an', the cry of lament for the dead Adonis, whose blood, to quote Farrer's excellent phrase, 'Flames yearly back again to light in the pulsing scarlets of *A. fulgens* and *A. coronaria*', both inhabitants of this part of the world. In this case the 'o' will be short rather than long.

The great woolly Pasque flowers are now more often placed

in a separate genus *Pulsatilla* than in *Anemone* where they used
to be included, being readily distinguished by their long
feathery seeds. The Pasque flower is now *Pulsatilla vulgaris*
and the two alpine species *P. vernalis* and *P. alpina;* the white
form is the type, while the dazzling sulphur-yellow one is
regarded as a subspecies of *P. alpina* under the awkward name
apiifolia rather than the much better known one of *sulphurea.*
Most of this genus, particularly *P. alpina*, make a thick, almost
wooden root, consequently they greatly resent disturbance and
if you want to collect them from the Alps you should take
seed or young seedlings if you can find them.*

Pulsatilla vulgaris is actually a native plant of this country
and can be found along the Devil's Dyke near Cambridge.
It follows particularly limestone and the old mortar broken
down from Roman works. The flowers are violet and starry
in the wild forms and gradually rise from great woolly clumps
until they open six inches or more high to reveal the mass of
golden stamens. Some of the garden forms are even finer, deep
purples, crimsons, pinks and even an albino, and they seem to
be larger and fuller in flower. Their first flowers should open
in mid-March in a favourable season and continue for a month
till mid-April. After that the stems lengthen and the great
silvery mops of feathery seeds appear rising above the fern-like
foliage, a decoration which will last half the summer in a
corner of the rock garden, so that one reaps a double reward.
These are most tolerant plants which should be in every garden.
Although preferring the chalk, they will grow well without
it. Like other anemones they thrive best in a sunny position.
The finest of all is probably the subspecies *grandis* of *P. halleri*,
and the form known as 'Budapest' – a glorious pale silvery-blue
with an enormous flower and a big yellow centre – probably
belongs to this species from eastern Europe, and in this the
leaves hardly develop till after the flowers.

Although abundant in the Alps we very rarely see *Pusatilla
alpina*, its subsp. *apiifolia*, or *P. vernalis* thriving in English
gardens and I have never found the factor which prevents

* They are not strictly tuberous, but seem to fit in best here.

them. *P. alpina* flowers later than *P. vulgaris* and has a large creamy-white flower on stems a foot high, attractive fern-like foliage and large tousled silvery seed heads. *P. vernalis* is a plant of the higher Alps and is even more lovely; the flowers are as early as those of *P. vulgaris* and in bud resemble a great downy egg covered with silver and golden hairs, sparkling from the dew, opening to a most beautiful opalescent goblet rising out of the nest of silky foliage. Even if you cannot grow this plant satisfactorily you should read Farrer's wonderful description of it in the 'English Rock Garden' and hope one day to see it in the Alps where it is common enough. In spite of Farrer's remarks, however, on the 'ease' of cultivation it is still a very uncommon plant in English gardens, while its native cousin the Pasque flower is common enough.

CROCUSES

The crocus season opens in the early autumn and runs right through till spring, but the greatest richness of species is in the winter and wonderful they are opening with each gleam of sun, or even sometimes in grey muggy weather without sun, for it seems to be the warmth rather than the actual sunlight which opens them. Indoors they will open flat, destroying some of their natural cup-shaped charm. The detail in the flower of the wild species and a few of the smaller hybrids, the beautiful and variable feathering on the petals often in deepest purple and maroon, make an exciting contrast with the basic tones, while the feathery scarlet stigmas of some species and the yellow throats to the flowers show up brilliantly when they open and well repay a careful look; many of the petals too, have a glistening satin sheen. It follows from this that crocuses grown raised up from the ground either in sinks or in a bulb frame are doubly rewarding, especially for elderly people, and we enjoy some each winter grown in both ways. Those in the sinks we replace each year, planting out the old corms in May or, if dried off, in September, but the rarer species in the bulb frame we leave undisturbed and they have a good summer baking in situ with their glass covering.

The autumn-flowering species grade into the winter flowerers and the winter flowerers into the spring, and for the crocus specialist there is a multitude of species to choose from. This year the mauve globes of *C. speciosus* opened late owing to a dry early autumn and some are still in flower right into the beginning of December, although *C. kotschyanus*, the warm lilac-mauve crocus with the golden spots at the base, which used so aptly to be called *C. zonatus*, finished with October. These are both still relatively cheap to buy and will spread freely in most gardens from seed if planted in the shrub border or even in the grass. They look well in the rock garden, but among the choicer alpines or in the bulb frame may prove too invasive. Unfortunately the selected bluer forms of *C. speciosus* such as 'Cassiope' and 'Oxonian' have not proved so vigorous or long lasting in most gardens. The Spanish *C. nudiflorus*, with its deeper purplish-mauve narrow flowers without any leaves and its curious and desirable habit of tillering out new bulbs on the ends of stolons, is more rarely seen but is a good plant where it will settle, flowering well on into November. It usually does best in damp positions. In the bulb frame we grow the lilac-mauve *C. longiflorus* and the beautifully feathered *C. medius* and the more delicate pale lilac *C. tournefortii* from the Greek islands, while sometimes we get a flower or two from the white *C. boryi* or its even larger flowered Greek relation *C. niveus*, a snow-white flower of great magnificence; if only it grew and increased better! These flower through October and November.

For December, *C. laevigatus* from Greece is the most reward- ing species. The small lilac flowers are rather globular and delightfully feathered with deeper purple on the outside. The best form is var. *fontenayi* but they are infinitely variable. They do need a warm position where the corms can be well ripened in summer. The same applies particularly to *C. imperati* which flowers early in January, or often in December. I have been able to pick flowers on Christmas or New Year's Day. The flowers are quite large; when closed they are pale buff-yellow veined prominently with deeper purple, but when open they show the three inner petals and the inside of the flower which is a bright lilac-mauve veined with deeper mauve with a yellow throat and a bright orange-red stigma. In my older garden I grew them at the foot of a cherry and in my present one they grow at the foot of a myrtle and seem to do well with the root competition which keeps them dry in summer. At the same time, either in one of the sinks or the bulb frame, the orange *C. korolkowii* from Afghanistan flowers and seems to be a vigorous species. It is heavily feathered with purplish-mahogany on the outside and a handsome flower.

In January and February we have a wealth of species but the most valuable of all are the little 'Tommies,' *C. tomasinianus*, which flower so early and spread so freely. There are wonderful naturalised masses of this in some gardens such as the hundred yard long border of it at Highdown in the warm chalk above Worthing. They give the same kind of effect as the delightful little wild *Crocus vernus*, that pale ghost of the Alps appearing through the melting snows and then opening to show its colour. Outside the Tommies are pale suede-like mauvish-blue, but inside they are a bright lilac-mauve. There are several named varieties of which the best are 'Whitewell Purple', a rich purplish-mauve and a larger flower than the type, 'Barr's Purple', a rich purplish-lilac inside, and 'Taplow Ruby' the nearest to a good deep pink of the named forms. But from any mass of seedlings one can nearly always pick out richer coloured seedlings than the type, also some with a deeper coloured marking near the tips of the petals which may have crossed with an early flowering form of *C. vernus*.

Among the other species of late January and early February are *C. biflorus* mauve and lilac with fine feathering, *C. dalmaticus* a rare uniform lilac-mauve, *C. susianus*, *C. balansae* and *C. olivieri* for the oranges. These last are hot, fiery and dramatic in their colour and perhaps the most intensely brilliant of all is *C. olivieri* which can also be distinguished by its very wide leaves. *C. balansae* and *C. susianus*, the 'Cloth of Gold', are tinged outside with the deepest mahogany, like a well-cared for piece of furniture.

30

Early February brings also the numerous forms of *Crocus chrysanthus* from the eastern end of the Mediterranean, from the mountains of northern Greece, Parnassus and the Pindus and from Turkey and the Levant. The wild type is a good orange but variable, and from natural seedlings and crossings, possibly some with other species such as *C. biflorus* var. *weldenii* or *C. aerius*, a vast range of colour forms has been developed extending from good whites with purple featherings to creams, yellows, oranges, mauves and blues. The late Mr E. A. Bowles at Myddelton House, by Enfield, was a pioneer in this and named a fine series after the smaller and more brightly coloured birds. The good work was carried on in Holland by the Hoog family of the famous bulb firm of Van Tubergen and they named their finest yellow seedling 'E. A. Bowles'. It is still one of the best. Others are still being raised in Holland and each year brings new ones into the really quite long lists of the bulb catalogues. With dwarf irises of the *Reticulata* section they give the main effect in our winter bulb sinks, while in the open in a sunny well drained place they are often persistent and can be mingled to make a true 'Primavera' with dwarf irises, cyclamen, snowdrops and snowflakes and winter aconites. Some of my favourites are:

'Blue Pearl', pale silvery-blue with a yellow throat, silvery-blue outside.

'Cream Beauty', pale creamy-yellow, free-flowering.

'E.A. Bowles', deep butter-yellow.

'Gipsy Girl', deep yellow, heavily streaked with purplish-chocolate outside.

'Goldilocks', deep golden-yellow, feathered lightly with bronze outside.

'Ladykiller', purplish-mauve bordered white outside, inside white.

'Saturnus', yellow with purplish-blue markings outside. One of the earliest.

'Snow Bunting', white with creamy flush on outside and feathered with dark lilac, inside white.

'Sultan', dark purplish-mahogany with white margin
outside, inside white with deep yellow throat.
'Warley White', large flowers, outside pale cream heavily
suffused with dark bluish-purple, inside
white with yellow throat.
'Zwanenburg Bronze', very deep bronzy-gold outside,
deep yellow inside, one of the
most free-flowering.

Closely following on the *chrysanthus* varieties are the various
varieties of *C. sieberi*, also from the mountains of Greece and
Crete and these are mostly true wild varieties. The one from
Crete known as *versicolor* or *heterochromos* is surely among the
loveliest of all crocuses as it flowers by the melting snow on the
White Mountains; it is basically a white flower with deep
purplish-maroon feathering and markings, but it is so variable
that no two seem to be quite alike; the commonest form is the
Attic variety which has a rather globular deep mauve flower
with the strong yellow throat so distinctive of this species.
'Violet Queen' is a selected form of it with smaller but deeper
mauve colour, while the beautiful *tricolor* from Mount Chelmos
has a large flower with a white band between the yellow throat
and the mauve upper part of the petals. I have seen large
clumps of this outside on a stony bank in the Cotswolds otherwise most of these *sieberi* crocuses seem safer in a bulb frame or
alpine house. Mr Bowles, however, used to grow outside quite a
large group of his much prized white form known as 'Bowles's
White' and regarded it, rightly I think, as the finest white-
flowering spring crocus.

All these crocuses come from the Mediterranean and Asia
Minor and like to be well baked during the summer if possible.
Otherwise they are no more difficult to grow than the ordinary
yellow, white or mauve hybrids that decorate our parks.
These species are well worth planting all over the rock garden
and at the edge of narrow borders by the house. Their fine
grass-like foliage does little harm in the summer and often acts
as a pleasant foil to other flowers such as the trumpets of

(*Above*) *Anemone blanda*. The deep blue variety *atrocoerulea* is the form to choose. (Reginald A. Malby & Co.)

(*Below*) *Anemone nemorosa* 'Allenii', which has larger flowers than the type. (H. Smith)

(*Above*) *Pulsatilla vernalis*, a lovely species from the higher Alpine meadows. (Reginald A. Malby & Co.)

(*Below*) *Crocus chrysanthus* 'E. A. Bowles', still one of the finest of the deep yellow varieties. (Reginald A. Malby & Co.)

Gentiana acaulis, making them seem more natural and meadow-like than when grown alone.

Pans of crocuses are also most attractive in the alpine house and even in the house but no attempt to force them should be made. The flowers open wide in the sun or when brought into a warm room, while in the bulb frame the choicer species should thrive and form large clumps. They do, however, need protection from mice. In the woodland and in the garden I prefer to keep the Dutch yellows separate from the large mauve and white Dutch varieties, but again this is a matter of taste. The old varieties, 'Purpureus Grandiflorus' and 'Negro Boy' for the deep purple, and 'Kathleen Parlow' or 'Jeanne d'Arc' for the whites, are still worth growing. They have been developed far from the *Crocus vernus* of the Alps. There is also one early variety 'Vanguard', slenderer than the later Dutch ones, pale mauve, following close on the little Tommies and usually opening in February.

CYCLAMEN

There always seems to me something faintly artificial about the species *Cyclamen*, yet they have a charm and a distinction that is very pleasing. It is hard to describe exactly in what it lies, partly perhaps in the dainty swan-like pose of the ballerina flowers, a head-dress fit for a fairy queen. No less attractive are the leaves, which in some species appear after the flowers and are ivy-like, marbled with silver.

The season of hardy cyclamen begins, like that of the crocus species, in early autumn or even late summer but often a few flowers of *C. europaeum* and *C. neapolitanum* with its infinite variability in shape and markings are a constant delight all through the winter. E. A. Bowles, a great authority on the genus, once wrote most aptly, 'it pays rent for eleven months out of the twelve', and there are few plants that can equal this. August is in this case the twelfth month when it is dormant and should be given a mulch of sifted leaf mould unless the trees above have already provided this. Unfortunately the nomenclature of the hardy cyclamen has been much confused in the past, largely owing to the lack of precision of earlier authors, even including the great Linnaeus, in describing the species to which they referred or quoting among their references names now associated with other species. Many authorities now consider that the correct name for *C. europaeum* should be *C. purpurascens*, appropriate because of the purplish-crimson of the underneath of the leaf, while *C. neapolitanum* should be called *C. hederifolium*, again quite appropriate owing to the ivy-like shape of its leaves.

Equally hardy outside and often lasting in flower later into the early winter is *C. cilicium*, a smaller and more delicate flower than *C. neapolitanum*. Like that plant, the earliest flowers appear without the leaves. They are pale rose-pink with a prominent red spot at the base, which is constricted but without the auricles of *neapolitanum*. The leaves are rather small, rounded with silvery markings. Close also to *C. neapolitanum* are *C. africanum*, more tender with larger leaves, and *C. graecum* which has striking rounded velvety leaves with a horny margin and round instead of knobbly tubers. It is also rather tender but grows well in a limestone wall at Highdown where the tubers are tucked in underneath the rocks.

Later in the early winter about November, *C. cyprium* flowers. It is smaller than *C. neapolitanum* but has the same kind of auricles round the base of the flower and a strong spicy scent. It is, however, tender and is usually treated as an alpine house plant although we are now trying it also in the bulb frame. It grows in Cyprus under the cedar trees of the old forest.

During January and February *Cyclamen coum* produces little flowers of most vivid, almost fierce pink, more dumpy than the swan winged flowers of *C. neapolitanum* but rather stronger in colour. The earliest and brightest form seems to be the one with unmarbled leaves, but the one that used to be known as *C. hiemale* is also early and usually a good colour. Both those with plain and those with marbled leaves are now placed under *C. coum* and this includes those sometimes known as *C. ibericum*, *C. vernum*, *C. orbiculatum* and *C. atkinsii*. They are very hardy and should be established in a warm and sunny place where they will be fairly dry in summer. For this reason they do well in a bulb frame and in pans for the alpine house where the summer watering can be restricted.

For the bulb frame or alpine house the smaller species are well worth growing such as *C. balearicum*, which has almost white leaves and white flowers, and a little later *C. creticum* which also has white flowers with a spicy acrid scent and taller stems and ivy-shaped or rounded toothed leaves. The flowers are long and graceful rather like those of the later-flowering *C. repandum*. Unfortunately neither of these can be reckoned as generally hardy outside in England. Nor probably can *C. pseudibericum* which resembles *C. coum* in flower but is larger and usually a richer deeper purple with a pronounced blotch at the base. In warm areas it is, however, worth experimenting by planting one or two tubers in a very warm rather dry spot. The progeny of the original introduction to Van Tubergen's is still the finest form with the tallest flowers and the brightest colour, but it is rarely seen and the forms much more often grown are those more recently introduced from South-West Turkey by various expeditions. It is indeed one of the finest species for the alpine house or bulb frame and rivals *C. libanoticum* which flowers about the same time. In this the flowers are a good pale blush-pink with a deeper coloured blotch at the base. The finest group of this I ever saw was growing in the soil under the central staging of the greenhouse in the garden of Lewis Palmer, and there was more than a square yard of it covered with flower.

The true wild form of *C. persicum*, so common in the mountains of Cyprus and again in the Lebanon, is one of the finest bulbs we can grow for the alpine house or slightly heated greenhouse where it will flower throughout February and March. Again it is very variable, the white forms being tipped with purple while the pink ones vary from a charming shell-pink to quite a deep pink, each flower with a deeper blotch at the base. They stand up above the marbled leaves to six inches or more and have so much more charm and grace than the large winter-flowering hybrids which have been developed from them for our warmer houses. I well remember one lovely drive up into the mountains of Lebanon on a sunny day early one April when all the loose limestone walls at the edge of the road were thick with *Cyclamen persicum* mingled with the single scarlet Turban ranunculus *R. asiaticus*.

C. repandum from Corsica and Italy sometimes just comes into our period in the alpine house, but hardly outside. Its wavy flowers make it one of the most beautiful of the species. Out of doors it grows best in a little shade, but this is not necessary in the alpine house. There is a rare white form, and I once found corms of it in a valley full of these cyclamen in Corsica where it grew on open moorland, but unfortunately the white form is rare in cultivation. Still, the pink is lovely enough for most of us.

All the cyclamen, with the possible exception of *C. libanoticum*, are easy of cultivation and seem able to maintain themselves, their corms waxing in width and stature each year, in the driest of situations round the boles of ancient trees – even cedars or beeches, under which little else will grow. The only condition they will not tolerate is a water-sodden one without drainage.

IRIS

The sturdy little *Iris histrioides* shares with the 'Stylosa' the honour of January flowering. In colour it is very similar, perhaps slightly bluer, more a rich, bright royal blue with only a faint tint of mauve in it, but it lacks the delicate appearance of the 'Stylosa'. It is a stout little fellow, as broad as high, erect and prim as a miniature oak, and seems able to withstand the wind and quite a hard frost unbowed, although a cloche when it is in flower will protect it from becoming dashed and weather-beaten with mud. The flowers are four inches across, divided very definitely into three segments which grow outwards almost at right angles to the short stem. The standards are upright as usual. The end of the fall is rather larger than in

Iris reticulata and a brilliant golden blotch marks the end of the golden streak which runs down its centre. This streak of brilliant colour is flanked by attractive tiger fleckings of dark and light colour.

Although *Iris histrioides* is not a difficult plant to grow in a well-drained position, it has remained rare and rather expensive, and I think this is partly due to its lack of permanency in this country in the form of big bulbs. After flowering, often a mass of small bulbs are produced and these need to be grown on for several years to flowering size. This iris comes from northern Asia Minor and its centre of distribution appears to be round Amasia which is in Turkey, south of the Black Sea. It extends into northern Persia. The variety described as *major* is slightly larger than the type and is probably the most satisfactory to grow. Like all irises from Asia Minor it needs very good drainage, and a thorough baking in summer.

Iris histrioides is a rather stouter plant than its close relative *Iris histrio*, which does not seem to grow well in English gardens. Its variety *aintabensis*, however, flowers even earlier than *I. histrioides major*, generally in January. It has done well outside at Highdown at the foot of the chalk cliff and has flowered for us in most years in my bulb frame. It is a lovely little plant, a bright turquoise-blue with golden markings, slenderer than *I. histrioides* and less heavily spotted than most forms of *I. histrio;* also it does not make the long leaves at the time of flowering, which that species often grows. It comes from farther north than the other forms of *I. histrio* and is probably quite hardy.

Another great treasure in this section is the comparatively recent hybrid 'Katharine Hodgkin', raised by the late E. B. Anderson between *I. histrioides major* and *I. danfordiae*, a deep yellow-flowered species. It is now just coming into the nurserymen's lists and seems to be a stronger grower, while its flowers show the sturdy poise of *I. histrioides major* but have a colour almost unique in the genus – pale sea-green blue overlaid with yellow and cream and strongly marked with gold, a flower difficult to describe.

The finest yellow among these dwarf irises of this section is undoubtedly *I. winogradowii* from the Caucasus and Georgia and I have seen it doing well enough outside but unfortunately it has remained a rare and expensive bulb. It has flowers in form like *I. histrioides*, but in colour a clear lemon-yellow; they are only three or four inches tall. Bertram Anderson grew it successfully on top of a wall in the Cotswolds where it got superb summer drainage. *I. danfordiae* is also deep yellow and flowers with the *Reticulatas* but is a dumpy flower without any proper standards, while after flowering the bulbs tend to split up into masses of little rice grains which take some years to reach flowering size again.

Another very attractive and sturdy little plant which often flowers in February is Iris 'Sindpers', a cross between *Iris aucheri* (formerly *sindfarensis*) and *I. persica;* the flowers are a pale electric blue-green with gold markings. Unfortunately, though, it is a very rare and expensive plant but I have in recent years seen good specimens in nurserymen's hands.

Iris reticulata, with its delicate form and rich velvet-purple flowers with their golden markings, is among the most delightful and easy to grow of the spring bulbs and flowers in February or early March. In recent years large numbers of selected forms and hybrids between *I. reticulata* and *I. histrioides major* or *I. bakeriana* have become available and are mostly good strong growers with larger flowers than the type. They are indeed one of the great additions to the winter garden and have become nearly as cheap as *reticulata* itself. They have quite superseded the older 'Hercules' and 'J.S. Dijt' and even 'Cantab'. They have also greatly extended the range of colour in this group. Among those I particularly like are:

'Blue Veil', bright sky-blue with contrast between the falls and standards.
'Clairette', bicolor, falls gentian-blue with white flaking, standards sky-blue.
'Harmony', deep sky-blue with golden stripe on falls. One of the most free-flowering.

'Jeanine', dark violet-purple with gold markings on falls,
      scented.
'Joyce', clear sky-blue, rather similar to 'Harmony'.
'Royal Blue', fine dark blue with broad falls.
'Spring Time', striking bicolor, falls dark violet-blue with
      white central markings, standards pale
      blue. Seems to persist well both in garden
      and bulb frame.
'Violet Beauty', deep violet with conspicuous orange
      crest on falls.
'Wentworth', purplish-blue, like a larger *I. reticulata*.

All these are excellent grown in pans for the alpine house but
no attempt must be made to force them.

Rarely seen now and difficult in pots is *Iris planifolia*, which
used to be known as *I. alata*, one of the Juno irises and very
early to flower in December or January. It grows wild and
vigorously, however, in North Africa and I well remember
seeing little Arab boys selling great bunches of it in early
December in the streets of Constantine in the centre of Algeria.
I thought, at first, that they were stylosa irises; would that it
would flower like that for us in England! But the flowers are
larger and more floppy than the stylosas and the falls slightly
fringed at their edges. They are deep mauve in colour with a
strong orange crest to the falls.

Some of the other dwarf Juno irises such as the forms of
I. persica, *I. nicolai* and *I. caucasica* are early flowering and
fascinating, but they are so touchy and difficult to grow successfully for long that they can only find a little space here. They
are for the real connoisseur. Never a drop of water must be
given over their leaves. The stylosa irises, forms of *I. unguicularis*
are, of course, among the very best of winter-flowering plants
but they have already been discussed in the Introduction.

MINIATURE AND EARLY DAFFODILS

Like the crocuses, the daffodil season also starts in the late autumn and early winter with a very peculiar group of three species from the Mediterranean and South Italy. These are *Narcissus elegans*, *N. serotinus* and *N. viridiflorus*. All these have much reduced cups, shallow and saucer-shaped, and rush-like or flat narrow leaves, and are unfortunately very shy of flowering in English gardens although they do so sometimes from freshly collected bulbs. They certainly need a stronger summer baking and should only be attempted in pans or in the bulb frame. *N. viridiflorus* is perhaps the easiest to flower and is a very interesting addition to the range of green flowers with its star-like flowers and small white centre. The other two are whiter in flower.

In December and January, again from pots and bulb frame, come the lovely Mediterranean forms of the Hoop-petticoat daffodils *N. bulbocodium* and *N. cantabricus*. Their nomenclature is very confused and I follow here the slightly complicated naming of Dr Fernandes, the Spanish expert on the group. Probably the best of the early ones is the pale lemon-yellow *N. romieuxii* from the Atlas Mountains, now regarded as a subspecies of *N. bulbocodium*. It is a very pretty flower about three or four inches high, delicate and almost translucent but yet tough enough to last in flower for a week or more in December or January. The same characters apply to the snowy white *monophyllus* from the south of Spain, Gibraltar and North Africa. They are now regarded as a subspecies of *N. cantabricus*. Here belong the forms sometimes known as *clusii* and *foliosus* but most have more than one leaf. A most unusual and beautiful white variety with the mouth of the cup recurring and forming a ruff an inch or more across, called var. *petunioides*, has recently been introduced and is well worth growing if you can get it. In all these the anthers are slightly deeper in colour and emerge beyond the broad flaring cup to curl slightly upwards, and the flowers have a delicate scent. Some good hybrids have also been raised recently between the yellow *romieuxii* and the white *monophyllus* and these are slightly larger in flower but still open as early in the year. These are called 'Muslin', 'Nylon' and 'Tarlatan' and are gradually

Crocuses at Kew. (H. Smith)

Iris histrioides major in early March. (D. Wilkie)

(*Above*) *Narcissus cantabricus* var. *petunioides*, a very early white variety. (J. E. Downward)

(*Below*) *Narcissus asturiensis*, a good form and usually the first dwarf daffodil to flower. (J. E. Downward)

(*Above*) *Galanthus* 'Straffan', one of the finest snowdrops for forming large masses. On the right are *Crocus tomasinianus*. (J. E. Downward)

(*Below left*) *Leucojum vernum*, the largest winter snowflake. (J. E. Downward)
(*Below right*) *Tulipa kaufmanniana*, one of the earliest tulips to flower. (Reginald A. Malby & Co.)

(*Top left*) *Eranthis hyemalis*, the common winter aconite. (Reginald A. Malby & Co.)

(*Top right*) *Scilla bifolia*, usually the earliest blue squill. (H. Smith)

(*Left*) *Chionodoxa luciliae*, which can spread freely into lovely blue drifts. (H. Smith)

finding their way into the general lists of bulbs for they are such good plants.

The ordinary hoop-petticoat naturalises well in grass and on banks, but is not successful in dry conditions. It is a beautiful sight each year in February or early March at Wisley where it makes a golden expanse all over the Alpine meadow, a grass slope near the rock garden and by the paths of the old wild garden. The same effect has been achieved in both the Savill and the Valley gardens in Windsor Great Park by scattering seed widely. I regard these effects as among the great achievements of British horticulture, although of course one needs time as well as a suitable site to achieve them; but nevertheless one can start in quite a small way. The time of flowering varies very much with the season, but the display extends over quite a long period: in some years it is best in mid-February, in others not until March and very occasionally not till early April. Much of the effect has been obtained by planting originally several different forms of the hoop-petticoats such as var. *citrinus* and var. *conspicuus* and var. *obesus*, a larger fatter flower, and these have crossed together to give hybrid vigour to the plantings. In Spain one year in the Gredos Mountains, although not till early June, I saw a great moorland, miles of it, covered with these little daffodils in full flower, a sight I have not forgotten. One important proviso is that the grass should not be cut before about mid-June so as to allow the seeds to mature and scatter.

Slightly preceding these in flower is *Narcissus cyclamineus* which is a deeper richer yellow and one of the most beautiful of all Narcissus species. The corona (cup) is long and tubular, while the outer segments recurve completely, forming a tall crown above the cup. One writer compared it to the 'ears laid back of a kicking horse'. It is especially a moisture lover and grows magnificently beside the ditches and damp banks at the edge of the old wild garden at Wisley and has naturalised itself there freely. Occasionally among them one will find a larger flower than the type with the petals less recurved, and these are usually well worth separating out and preserving as they are probably naturally occurring hybrids between *N. cyclamineus* and a small trumpet daffodil such as *N. asturiensis*, the smallest trumpet which used to be known most appropriately as *N. minimus*, and so the hybrids are called 'Minicycla'.

Almost as early flowering, the little *N. asturiensis* is a perfect miniature trumpet only two or three inches tall. The flower is a good golden-yellow and the mouth is deeply indented, almost frilled, the throat being rather narrow. Unfortunately the stem is rather weak and although the plant is very hardy and the flowers fairly frost-resisting, after rain it tends to lie down so is perhaps better grown through a very low spreading mat of silvery-grey foliage such as an *Acaena*. It requires better drained conditions than the *bulbocodiums* and *cyclamineus* and also more summer ripening. Some of the slightly larger trumpets, such as *N. minor* and its more solid yellow variety *pumilus* and its straw-yellow double *eystettensis*, better known as Queen Anne's double daffodil, and our own wild daffodil *N. pseudonarcissus* the Lent Lily, and its deeper yellow sub-species *obvallaris* will also sometimes flower towards the end of February or during March, although in a late season they may not come out till April. They are stronger growing and excellent for naturalising.

Undoubtedly the dwarf narcissi, particularly the smaller ones, are now becoming more popular as the hybrids get larger and redder. Unfortunately the smallest tend to be nearly as expensive in most catalogues as the largest and the price may well be in inverse proportion to their size. Still many people find a bowl, or a pan in a bowl, of dwarf daffodils more satisfactory for the dining-table decoration than the larger ones as they can see their friends easily across the table above it. These bulbs, however, must not be forced with any heat. For this purpose, and also in the alpine house or outside, the little Angel's Tears, *Narcissus triandrus*, are excellent and among the prettiest and most graceful of the smaller daffodils. At the Savill Garden in Windsor Great Park there is a naturalised meadow of them. They generally flower in early to mid-March, but again this varies much with the season. The flowers of the type which used to be called var. *albus* vary from a pure white to creamy-white and the bell-like cup is pendulous and half as long as the outer segments. In the var. *loiseleurii* it is larger. The Angel's Tears daffodils are widespread in Spain and I have seen them there growing and flowering in running water as the snow melted higher up the mountain. There are several stories of the origin of the name. It was derived from a guide called 'Angelo' who went with Peter Barr who first introduced it. After climbing for a long time he was very tired and burst into tears and there was found this daffodil. Another version of the story says that he burst into tears on being sent back up the mountain to bring it down.

Unfortunately most of the jonquils and the poeticus daffodil bulbs flower too late for our winter period, but some of the hybrids of both *N. cyclamineus* and *N. triandrus* often flower before the end of February. One of the best is very aptly named 'February Gold' and we have often had it in flower in that month. About a foot tall, it is a good yellow with a fairly short cup. Other crosses between *N. cyclamineus* and the larger trumpet daffodils include 'Bartley' and 'Peeping Tom' both of which have very long trumpet-like cups and flower very early. Both are a very deep yellow and they are almost indistinguishable. 'Jana' is another good yellow which flowers very early and it is rather dwarfer than 'Bartley'. Sometimes that lovely trio 'Dove Wings', 'Charity May' and 'Jenny' will flower before the end of our period, but more often they come into early April. That very pretty little bicolor hybrid called 'Jack Snipe' with long yellow crown and white petals will, however, often flower early and is very lovely in pans for the alpine house.

N. watieri is a very charming miniature daffodil of the Jonquil section and usually the earliest of this group to flower. It has snow-white flowers and comes from high up in the bleak Atlas Mountains. It is hardy enough but, as might be expected, requires a good summer ripening. It cannot, however, be claimed as a vigorous or freely increasing plant in English gardens, but it is so beautiful a flower that it is worth the expense of buying a few bulbs from time to time. The flowers are starlike with short coronas and bloom singly on stems no more than a few inches tall.

For culture in bowls in bulb fibre a few daffodils which will flower by Christmas and during January are very valuable, and the earliest are nearly always the Polyanthus narcissi: the incredibly sweet-scented 'Scilly Isles White' closely followed by the yellow and orange 'Soleil d'Or' and the white and lemon 'Grande Monarque' and a little later 'Cragford', a Poetaz narcissus with bunches of orange-red cups backed by creamy-white petals over two inches across which even flowers well grown in damp shingle or in moist pebbles. Among the trumpets the earliest is usually the old 'Golden Harvest', followed by the finer 'Rembrandt', but with the modern methods of pre-cooling and preparation many of the later varieties can be brought into flower early, even for Christmas. But these are still more expensive than ordinary bulbs.

SNOWDROPS AND SNOWFLAKES

There is no other flower that I know that presents the ice-cold glistening white of the snowdrops. They couldn't be more aptly named. They are like the drops of a chandelier of ice, whitened with frost and glistening in the weak sun of winter.

The common snowdrop needs no further description from me, but there is also a certain number of species which are well worth growing and seem still to be little known. Several of them have flowers rather larger than the common snowdrop, although of the same colour and pattern. Some of them even flower earlier than the common *Galanthus nivalis*.

The snowdrop season will be opened with *Galanthus reginae-olgae* from the slopes of Mount Taygetus in Greece, if one can obtain and then grow it. It is not quite so easy to grow as the common snowdrop, but it is worth a little effort since it flowers any time from October till January. The flowers are slightly larger than the ordinary snowdrop, rather egg-shaped, and the leaves are more glaucous with a silvery band down the centre and appear after the flowers. Probably it requires better drained conditions and more summer ripening than the ordinary snowdrops, but I have seen quite large patches in some gardens. It is easy in the bulb frame or the alpine house. It is followed in November-December by *G. corcyrensis* in which the leaves are partly developed at flowering time.

Another early flowering form is *G. byzantinus* which has much larger flowers than the type, often in January and early February. Many bulb growers supply *G. elwesii* for bulb bowls and naturalising and it is a very valuable species, flowering in February and March. The flowers are globular and rather large for a snowdrop. The inner segments of the flower are prominently marked with green, both at the cleft and at the base. They seem to like a sunnier position than the ordinary snowdrop.

Galanthus plicatus is one of the later species to flower. It is vigorous with large flowers, rather globular in bud, but in maturity the three outer segments tend to become reflexed, and to spread outwards giving it a distinctive form. The name is derived from the leaf, which is plicate, being folded backwards and lengthwise like a small closed fan, and rather glaucous. The finest form is probably 'Warham' which was collected and sent home by a soldier in the Crimean war. It is the only snowdrop to have received a First Class Certificate (their highest award) from the Royal Horticultural Society.

Galanthus graecus is one of the earliest to flower and on a chalky soil seems to increase very freely. It is easily recognised by the twisted glaucous leaves.

Many named and enlarged forms or hybrids of the ordinary snowdrop have been raised and are now obtainable. Some of the best are 'Atkinsii', 'Magnet', 'Sam Arnott' and 'Straffan', and these persist well and increase in many gardens. Like all snowdrops, the clumps are best lifted when they are just finishing flowering or even when they are still in flower and they never need to be dried off. 'John Gray' has probably the largest flower of all, a massive great globe, but it is still rare and expensive. It is a good grower and increases so it should be available more widely soon.

All snowdrops, with the exception of such Greek mountain forms as *G. reginae-olgae*, naturalise well in woods where the ground is not too light and not too dry. The wide drifts of snowdrops seem, however, to be confined to certain counties. Unfortunately the hungry Surrey sand is not one of them. The heavier soils and damper places seem to grow snowdrops better.

The name snowdrop is of German origin and is derived from 'Schneetropfen', the little pendants or eardrops worn in the sixteenth or seventeenth century. Old English herbalists such as Gerard called it the 'white bulbous violet' and mixed up snowdrops and snowflakes indiscriminately. Later English names, 'Candlemas Bells', 'Fair Maids of February' and 'White Ladies', were associated with the festival of Candlemas day, February 2nd, when a procession of white-robed maidens celebrated the feast of the Purification. The name *Galanthus* was given by Linnaeus. In some books the snowdrop is considered as a native plant and it has in some counties become very widespread. Though we cannot have any firm evidence it is more probable, however, that the snowdrop was brought over from Italy by the Romans and planted round their villas together with crocus, narcissus and periwinkle.

The Snowflakes, Leucojums, or more truly Leucoeion (the white violet), are less well known in English gardens, but they are no more difficult to grow than the snowdrops. The most satisfactory species is the commonest, *L. vernum*, and in a mild winter this will begin to flower in February and continue throughout March. The little white bell-like flowers are very like those of snowdrops but all the segments of the flower are equal in length and are suspended seemingly by a hair alone from much taller stems than the snowdrops. The leaves are a bright yellow-green, unlike the blue-green leaves of the snowdrops, and provide a pleasant foil to the flowers.

In addition the spring snowflake has a faint, although sweet and easily distinguished scent. It is valuable for its time of flowering and its grace and charm, characters which are not appreciated so much in the summer snowflake *L. aestivum*, which flowers in May and is inclined to be eclipsed by more garish beauties.

There are forms with yellow instead of green tips to the segments, distinguished under the varietal name *carpathicum*, and others with two flowers instead of one to the stem which are distinguished under the name var. *vagneri*, while there are some with both characters together which have not been distinguished separately. The finest naturalised planting of the spring snowflake that I have ever seen was at Crathes Castle, a cold garden near Aberdeen in the north-east of Scotland. It was lovely spreading among the bushes with only bare twigs above, like a patch of snow, but there are nearly as fine ones in some Sussex gardens such as Nymans.

The snowflakes increase readily and seem to appreciate ordinary border conditions, but do not do so well in hot dry places.

TULIPS

There are two groups of tulips which come well into our period, first are members of the *humilis* group from the mountains of north-west Persia and north-east Turkey; these are closely followed by the better known Water Lily tulips, forms of *Tulipa kaufmanniana* from Turkestan and central Asia. *T. humilis* is a very dwarf plant with quite large dumpy flowers almost the size and shape of a hen's egg, raised only a few inches off the ground, but they are very brilliant in colour, in shades of shocking pink or magenta or violet-crimson, some self coloured, others with a white eye and all with an egg-yellow centre. Probably no other winter-flowering plant has such a strong violent colour. In any warmth they will open wide to make a flat star. Some forms have been split off in the past as separate species – *T. pulchella* with flowers slightly later and pinkish-crimson on the inside and *T. violacea*, also from north Persia and Kurdistan with a definite violet-purple colour – but there are many intermediates between them. They are absolutely hardy and I remember that on a botanical trip in Persia with Paul Furse we found forms of the *T. violacea* type flowering soon after the snow had melted in a very cold windy area on the big mountain group to the south of Tabriz. Even so, they were taller and more graceful than the forms in cultivation. In this country, however, they seldom seem to be very permanent in the open ground, tending to rot off too readily during the summer, and should be lifted or grown in the bulb frame or in pans in the alpine house.

The Water Lily tulip is, however, for most gardens the earliest to flower, and also one of the finest. The flowers, which seem the toughest of all tulips, will brave the coldest March winds, closed and nestling in their glaucous leaves. Sometimes the earliest bloom towards the end of February. When the warm spell comes, their stems lengthen and they open wide, so wide sometimes that their flowers are almost flat and horizontal, flushed and luxuriant as a small water lily. The flowers are large and the petals several inches in length, are attractively pointed. They vary enormously in colour from palest cream to most brilliant scarlet. Probably the most typical form is a creamy-white, strengthening to yellow in blotches at the base of the petal. The outsides of the outer three petals are tinged, almost striped in some cases, with deep pink, while the inner segments are all flushed at the base.

The Dutch bulb growers have in recent years brought us great developments and variety in this group, some being hybrids with the later-flowering *T. fosteriana* and *T. greigii* which have given them larger flowers, several inches across; and in the case of the *greigii* hybrids, beautifully streaked or mottled blue-green leaves, a very decorative feature. The earliest to flower is appropriately known as 'The First' and has creamy flowers with a little red on the outside and a yellow centre. It is close to the wild type but a little larger. One can buy these tulips in a good mixture called the Peacock strain, or as named varieties. Some of the best have been named after musicians and writers, including:

(*Top left*) *Erythronium citrinum*, one of the earliest of the dog tooth violets. (Reginald A. Malby & Co.)

(*Top right*) *Tecophilaea cyanocrocus*, which has flowers of gentian blue. (H. Smith)

(*Right*) *Fritillaria acmopetala*, which has bells of jade green and maroon. (J. E. Downward)

(*Above*) *Helleborus niger*, the Christmas rose. (H. Smith)

(*Below*) *Helleborus atrorubens*, which often flowers by Christmas, the earliest of the Lenten roses. (J. E. Downward)

(*Top left*) *Primula edgeworthii* planted in a good vertical position where the crowns are protected from winter wet. (J. E. Downward)

(*Top right*) *Primula* 'Wanda' has most brilliant reddish purple flowers in late January or February. (Reginald A. Malby & Co.)

(*Right*) *Primula clarkei* has delicate bright pink flowers. (H. Smith)

(*Top*) *Saxifraga oppositifolia* 'Splendens', one of the finest forms with deep reddish purple flowers. (Reginald A. Malby & Co.)

(*Centre*) *Saxifraga* 'Faldonside' has bright yellow flowers and silvery foliage. (Reginald A. Malby & Co.)

(*Bottom*) *Viola septentrionalis*, one of the largest violets with white and blue flowers. (Reginald A. Malby & Co.)

Camellia reticulata 'Noble Pearl' one of the finest Chinese forms. (J. E. Downward)

The best almond, *Prunus* 'Pollardii'. (Reginald A. Malby & Co.)

(*Above*) *Prunus subhirtella autumnalis* 'Rosea', one of the indispensable plants for winter flowers. The twigs can be cut for the house. (J. E. Downward)

(*Right*) *Prunus × blireana*, an early hybrid between *Prunus* 'Pissardi' and an apricot and one of the best early pink cherries. (Reginald A. Malby & Co.)

(*Above*) *Daphne mezereum*, a fine specimen of the white form. (J. E. Downward)

(*Below*) *Daphne blagayana*. (Reginald A. Malby & Co.)

(*Right*) *Prunus triloba*

(*Below*) *Erica carnea*, the winter flowering heath. (Reginald A. Malby & Co.)

Hamamelis mollis, the witch hazel which often begins to flower in December. (Reginald A. Malby & Co.)

'Alfred Cortot', deep scarlet with a black base. Leaves
        mottled.
'Brilliant', scarlet with golden-yellow base.
'César Franck', carmine-red edged with yellow outside,
        deep yellow inside and early-flowering.
'Fritz Kreisler', deep coral-pink with a deeper yellow base
        and ivory white inside with a deeper flush.
        One of the taller varieties.
'Scarlet Elegance', bright scarlet and early-flowering.
'Shakespeare', salmon flushed and blended with scarlet
        and with a yellow base, a very subtle
        combination of colour and my favourite in
        the group.
'Stresa', deep yellow with orange-red streaks on outside.
        A very conspicuous flower in late February and
        March.

These tulips are not difficult to grow and are generally no more expensive than the May-flowering hybrids. Their flowers are nearly as large, and they come two or three months earlier. All tulips like a rest and a baking during the summer, and in most soils are best lifted in July and replanted in October. The Water Lily tulips may, however, be left in the soil and will often establish themselves and continue flowering from season to season. They are excellent also for the bulb frame and alpine house. They propagate easily from offsets, and also make bulbs several inches below the original bulbs at the end of droppers. So when lifting it is always worth while digging more deeply than the original bulb; even if this is only represented by the outer husk it is worth digging below for the dropper bulb. *T. kaufmanniana* comes from Turkestan in central Asia where it is well baked in the summer.

Another early-flowering tulip is *T. saxatilis* from Crete, a species which presents a curious combination of colours, most effective in a few situations but difficult to place. The flowers are pale pink, but not a warm rosy pink, rather a lilac-pink with a strong yellow blotch at the base of the petal. The foliage is not glaucous as in the majority of tulips, but a grass green, bright and shiny. With us it spreads freely, both from seed and from rather lengthy stolons at the end of which new bulbs are produced, and its area should be restricted like that of a fig. In any case there are never nearly as many flowers as one might expect from the amount of foliage. The best group I have seen was in the limestone wall at the base of the chalk cliff at Highdown – a very warm place.

High up in the middle Atlas Mountains in Algeria, I found in early spring a delicate little tulip, pale cream and yellow, growing up through clumps of yellow-flowering and grey-leaved helianthemum in glades among the few remaining patches of cedar forest. It was an attractive combination, though I fear in this country the tulip would flower too early for the helianthemum. It was *Tulipa primulina*, a species which was first collected by Elwes in eastern Algeria.

There are also two rather small-flowered white and creamy-yellow tulips which flower usually in March. These are *T. biflora* from southern Russia, each stem of which can carry as many as five flowers, whitish stained with green and sometimes a little crimson; and *T. turkestanica*, rather similar in colouring but a little larger in flower and generally more vigorous, again with several blooms to a stem.

The season of the great scarlet species of tulip is ushered in during the second half of March by *T. praecox*, which has stems eighteen inches tall and quite large scarlet flowers with a yellow and olive-green blotch at the base. Although not very often grown, it is a good starter for the really magnificent feast that the tulips give us in April and May.

A MISCELLANY OF BULBS AND TUBERS:
Winter Aconites, Scillas, Chionodoxas, Muscaris, Colchicums, Tecophilaeas, Puschkinias, Hyacinthus, Erythroniums and Fritillaries

The winter aconites are some of the earliest bulbs to flower and also some of the most resistant to a hard winter. They are lowly flowers, sitting close to the ground, the brilliant yellow buttercup-like flower being framed by a green ruff, cheekily like dog Toby or dignified like some old noble or bishop. On the whole aconites are rather cheeky little flowers more like Toby than the bishop! The common winter aconite (*Eranthis hyemalis*) is deservedly well known. It should be planted in large clumps or drifts and sometimes will take several seasons to establish itself and spread. It is very tolerant of life under the branches of deciduous trees or in spaces among the shrubs but always seems to establish best in heavier soils and in rather moist places. The flowers are about the size and form of a buttercup and it belongs to the order *Ranunculaceae*. Their yellow, though, is even brighter or at any rate seems so at the season in which they flower, January and February.

Less well known is the beautiful winter aconite from Asia Minor *Eranthis cilicica*, which flowers slightly later than our European winter aconite, but the flowers are slightly larger and the foliage is more finely divided and often has a bronzy tinge. It is a good plan to intermingle the two species in drifts for a longer succession of bloom. Then there is also a very fine hybrid between these two species with flowers larger than either of them, *Eranthis tubergenii* raised by that magnificent Dutch bulb firm Van Tubergen. Unfortunately it is still rather an expensive plant. The flowers are sterile and it is claimed that they last longer than the flowers of the species but it can only spread by breaking up the tubers. In an alpine house this hybrid has always attracted my attention when in flower and it deserves to become more popular. The best form of it has been named 'Guinea Gold'. It flowers slightly later and is a little deeper in colour. Its leaves also are tinted with bronze.

From Japan there comes a little species with white flowers, *Eranthis pinnatifida*, but it is not such a robust plant as either of the yellow species and is only rarely seen.

The scillas and chionodoxas I always think of together. Both are common, both are brilliant in colouring and both are first-rate garden plants. With flowers of brightest gentian-blue in February and March, the scillas are most valuable for planting in patches over the rock garden and will grow up happily through mats of other prostrate plants, though some say they do better without any other ground cover. The earliest to flower, usually in February, is *Scilla bifolia*. This plant bears two to six flowers on a stem three to six inches in height and is a native of the mountains of southern Europe and Asia Minor. Some forms are more robust than the type and have been named. The best are probably var. *praecox* which is the earliest to flower and has larger flowering stems and flowers of a good bright blue. If happily established it will often spread freely and combines well with the very early narcissus such as *N. asturiensis*. Var. *taurica* is the largest form with up to twelve flowers to a stem. The flowers are bright violet-blue with purplish anthers and the stems are reddish. Unfortunately this very desirable form has always been rare since it only increases slowly. There are also white and pink forms.

Even more brilliant, although it flowers a little later, is *Scilla sibirica*. The flowers are of a deeper blue, almost the blue of a good *Gentiana acaulis*, and are shaped like nodding starry bells. Both these species should be planted in autumn and left in position, when they should multiply. They are not, however, so suitable as the winter aconites for planting in grass. There are several varieties of this scilla for which qualities above those of the type are claimed, and certainly from time to time I have seen some which seemed extra fine. Probably the variety described as *atrocoerulea* ('Spring Beauty') is one to choose as it is the most vigorous. There is also a white form.

There is an interesting plant, too, possibly a natural hybrid, introduced from Persia by Messrs Van Tubergen and named *Scilla tubergeniana* which has very pale blue flowers with a darker blue stripe down the centre of each petal. It is one of the earliest bulbs to flower, generally in early February as early as *S. bifolia*, and stays in flower for quite a long time. In flower it resembles *Puschkinia scilloides* but has a much shorter stem. It also spreads freely. It is a good plant for pans in the alpine house but does not need protected treatment. An unusual and striking combination is *Scilla sibirica* and *Cyclamen coum* placed together in the rock garden. Peter Davis has reported a similar combination from the Lebanon.

Chionodoxas are equally valuable as very early-flowering bulbs. They are close to the scillas, the two genera only being differentiated by the bases of the petals which are joined together in chinodoxas instead of being separated as in scillas. The chionodoxas to choose are *C. luciliae* with bright blue flowers and white centres and *C. sardensis* with deeper gentian-blue flowers. They are very early and very resistant to cold as their name 'Glory of the Snow' indicates, for they flower on the mountains of Asia Minor at the edge of the melting snow. In both chionodoxas and scillas there are white varieties of all the main species, and an occasional pale pink one may be found, but it is generally a rather mauvish-pink in tone and lacks the almost strident beauty of the type. With anemones and hepaticas all these bulbs should be planted in drifts where they will quickly intermingle. None will clash, and some of the scillas and chionodoxas may hybridise to produce the chiono-scillas.

The hybrid group between *Chionodoxa luciliae* and *Scilla bifolia* is *chionoscilla allenii*. The flowers are a bright sky-blue. There is a very finely coloured variety called 'Fra Angelico' which always makes a good display in the alpine house at Wisley very early in the year but unfortunately it is rare and difficult to obtain. They closely resemble the chionodoxas, and the petals are joined together at the base. Mr Bowles in the spring book of his delightful trilogy recommends planting at the base of briar roses: only, one must be generous; a single scilla or even half a dozen only makes a bright dot in the garden which is restless without being beautiful. If one can only have six, better grow them in a pan or even a bowl of fibre.

The largest chionodoxa is *C. siehei* with a stem up to ten inches and sometimes as many as fifteen flowers to a stem, but generally they are fewer. Each may be one and a quarter inches across, violet-blue, almost prussian-blue, with a conspicuous white centre. It is unfortunate that this is such a rare plant. It seems to form clumps by division but does not spread by

seeding in the same way as do *C. luciliae* and *C. sardensis*.
C. gigantea, which appears at about the same time, has much
shorter stems than *C. siehei* but even larger flowers, generally a
pale lilac-blue with a small white centre. There are also good
pink and white forms of it.

The muscaris or grape hyacinths are less vivid in colour
but no less charming in the early spring garden a little later
than the scillas. Soft powder-blue ranging to deeper indigo,
they make the perfect underplanting for early cherries or
magnolias. They do not mingle so well with the scillas and
chionodoxas, being slightly outmoded by their brilliance.
In our light sandy soil in Surrey they increased faster than any
other bulb and the only attention they seem to require is to
lift the roots every few years and divide the bulbs. They mingle
well with drifts of the dwarf narcissi, *bulbocodium* and *triandrus*.
Their only disadvantage is the rather untidy masses of foliage
in the early summer but this is really little trouble and in the
rock garden it can be pulled away about June when it has died
back. It is not wise, however, to plant the ordinary blue grape
hyacinths in any position with other choice bulbs or alpines for
they may quickly overrun the whole area, spawning off little
bulbs and seedlings in all directions. The grape hyacinths are
unusual in that the flask-like bells are narrowed at both ends, so
that Farrer not inaptly referred to their 'characteristic Rugby-
football shape'. Most of the dusky dark indigo-blue flowered
species such as *M. latifolium* and *M. neglectum* and *M. paradoxum* belong to the later season but the dwarf *M. botryoides*
which has almost globular flowers, pale china-blue or pure
white, will usually flower about the middle of March. It is not a
spreader like *M. racemosum* or 'Heavenly Blue' and can be
admitted among the choicer bulbs.

One other little bulb that will come into our season is
Puschkinia scilloides, known sometimes as the striped squill.
It grows under the same kind of conditions as most chionodoxas
and scillas in eastern Turkey and western Iran. We found it in
the wettest conditions possible where the clay was given by the
snow water a sticky consistency like plasticine. It has, however,

a wide distribution extending from the Caucasus to the Lebanon. It is taller than most of the scillas and has very pale blue or whitish bell-like flowers, crowded together into a head. Each petal has a median darker greenish-blue streak. The whole colour effect is like a taller *Scilla tubergeniana* and it flowers in March in most seasons. There is also a fine white form.

The wild form of *Hyacinthus orientalis*, which is so sweetly scented, flowers more often in England in April rather than in March but there are two smaller species *H. amethystinus* from the Pyrenees and *H. azureus* from the mountains of Asia Minor which will flower usually in March. The former has tubular drooping flowers, a delicate shade of Cambridge porcelain-blue, by no means an amethyst-blue, and is one of the most beautiful and delicate of late winter-flowering bulbs. There is also a white form. *H. azureus* has a thickly clustered head, rather like that of a grape hyacinth, and flowers of a brilliant azure-blue. Mr Bowles recommended growing it with *Crocus aureus* for contrast.

None of the larger colchicums of the glossy catalogues flowers within our period, but among the heavily tessellated species *Colchicum variegatum* flowers in late October and through November – a very distinctive flower with a more distinct pattern and darker colouring than in any of the other species of this group. A plant of Greece and the Greek islands, it is best grown in a bulb frame where it can get some protection, although I have grown it successfully outside. The winter and early spring-flowering species are all smaller in flower and rarer in cultivation although, owing to recent collecting in the Middle East, a number of them can be seen in the alpine houses and bulb frames of Wisley and other botanic gardens or at early shows of the Alpine Garden Society and they are mostly lovely little plants. Perhaps the finest is the bunch-flowered white *C. brachyphyllum* from the Lebanon which often flowers in December and January. *C. kesselringii* from Turkestan and Afghanistan has flowers of unusual colouring, white with prominent lilac-mauve central streaks, but they are not large. *C. ancyrense* and *C. bifolium* with purplish-pink or white flowers, both from Turkey and north-west Persia, flower in the alpine house or bulb frame from January to March, but are unfortunately slow to raise from seed.

There is one other brilliant blue beauty which is a plant for the true connoisseur. I refer to the Chilean crocus *Tecophilaea cyanocrocus*. It has the real deep gentian-blue with a tinge of paler sky suffused to white towards the throat. It comes from the Chilean Andes around 10,000 feet where it has now become very rare, and when it does flower in this country does so in March or early April. A few examples may nearly always be seen at the spring R.H.S. shows 'pour encourager les autres'. It is undoubtedly difficult of cultivation and rare in the south of England, but there are gardens both in Norfolk and in the south of Ireland where it has established itself and flowered freely. It is even more brilliant in colouring, more vividly unreal and arresting than the scillas, having almost the blue of a *Gentiana verna*. Its peculiar name is derived from Tecophila the daughter of an Italian botanist. It is not, as I supposed at first, a tribute to some ancient Indian warrior chief.

Last in our miscellany we come to the erythroniums and fritillaries which, although less brilliant in colouring, for me have more charm and distinction than any of those genera mentioned earlier except perhaps the *Tecophilaea*. Erythronium leaves have a pleasant mottled glaucousness and their flowers have the grace and to some extent the form of miniature lilies, especially the cream and yellow North American species and varieties. The earliest to flower, generally beginning in mid-March, is our European Dog-Tooth Violet *E. dens-canis*, named dog-tooth from the tooth and claw-like appearance of a cluster of the bulbs. The flowers are pink, several inches across, nodding delicately on slender stems and slightly recurved like a lily, revealing the pleasant markings towards the centre. There are numerous varieties including a very fine white one. The Dog-Tooth Violet spreads freely with us and is attractive as clumps in the rock garden or as drifts underplanted below azaleas. They do not seem particular over conditions but their natural habitat is an open woodland and they usually grow best where it is not too dry. The west American varieties are slightly later in flowering, larger in flower but less robust in growth and propagation, at any rate with us. They are, however, very beautiful plants and it is unfortunate that they have remained relatively expensive in nurserymen's lists. Probably the best are *E. californicum* and *E. oregonum*, of which the well-known 'White Beauty' is one of the most attractive and makes large clumps in many gardens.

The flowers of this group range from creamy-white to deep yellow. Without marbling in the leaf, which is bright green, and with taller stems but smaller flowers of a deeper yellow is *E. tuolumnense*, a slightly unbalanced flower for its stem, but from it have been recently raised two more vigorous and larger-flowered hybrids named 'Kondo' and 'Pagoda' which I can strongly recommend. Probably *E. oregonum* or *E. californicum* was the other parent. The flowers of 'Kondo' are primrose-yellow and those of 'Pagoda' deep canary-yellow. Both grow up to a foot in height and have attractive marbled leaves. *E. revolutum* is the best of the pink ones and the flowers are a delightful combination of light pink inside and deeper pink outside and are a little larger than those of 'White Beauty'. It is known in its own country as the rose-pink Trout Lily and is very variable; consequently many names have been given at different times to particular forms. Those known as 'Pink Beauty' and var. *johnsonii* are the ones usually offered.

E. hendersonii also flowers at about the same time and is one of the more vigorous growers as well as being one of the most lovely in flower. These are unique in the genus in their colour, pale lilac with dark purple markings near the base and bright blue-mauve anthers. In the American species the leaves are less marbled than in the European but still there remains that tint of marbling which would make them decorative even if one had no flowers. All the erythroniums are excellent subjects for pans in the alpine house and will flower there a few weeks earlier than outside.

The bulbs of erythroniums should never be dried out, nor should they be planted in dry places. They seem particularly to appreciate ground which can be kept moist during the growing season. Once established they are best left to form large clumps, although these can be split up and replanted when the leaves are dying off about June.

The fritillaries are another group of great interest to the grower of choice bulbs. Grown outside, only a few such as *F. acmopetala* will flower within our season, the majority flowering in April or even early May. In pots or pans or in the bulb frame some may, however, be earlier. On 1st April in 1969, during the last R.H.S. Lily Conference Year, there was a co-operative exhibit of fritillaries in flower from many growers and eighty-five separate species were brought. Some had been in flower for a little time and been held back for the exhibition in cold storage; others, however, had been induced to open a little early with some extra heat, but as a genus they do not react well to attempts at forcing. This marvellous exhibit was the result of much enthusiasm and also much collecting in less known parts of Asia Minor in recent years, and many of the plants are not generally available except by exchange or from seed in various societies' seed lists.

The common Snake's Head Fritillary is as lovely as any but unfortunately usually flowers outside our winter period. *F. acmopetala*, with tall slender stems and quite large bells of maroon and green, is one of the most graceful and beautiful of the species which are generally available. Another is *F. crassifolia*, and in its best forms this is a real beauty with long bells of jade green and maroon and it seems to grow well in pans and in the bulb frame flowering in March or early April.

Herbs

CELANDINES, HEPATICAS, PERIWINKLES AND VIOLETS

Here is a miscellany of early flowers, mingling happily together like a Victorian posy. The celandines are some of the earliest to appear, and our common wild single golden celandine always gives me great pleasure as it grows in clumps below the white stems of the silver birches. It is in the wild garden that one can make especial use of such charming natives and they will seed and spread themselves about most freely. Some regard them as too invasive for the garden, and one famous gardener took me strongly to task for recommending them, so please feel warned if you only have a small garden, and grow only the special unspreading forms. But they are so lovely and so early to flower in the winter that I would not wish to be without them. Forms of celandine vary somewhat both in size of flower and intensity of colour, and there is a double kind but personally I prefer the single. The largest form is the Italian one, often called *major* or *grandiflorus* and it is nearly twice the size of the ordinary ones and makes clumps without spreading nearly so widely. There is also a creamy-white one, a primrose one and a deeper bronzy-orange than the type, and none of these is a spreader. The celandines are closely related to the buttercups but they have roots which are a mass of small tubers which readily break up to spread farther afield. The flowers are slightly deeper in colour than the average buttercup, often an inch and a half in diameter, and the petals have the buttercup sheen of finest satin. A fine January will bring the earliest celandines and they will continue through until March or even early April.

The hepaticas have at recurring intervals flirted with the genus *Anemone*, sometimes entering it, more often being relegated

59

to a separate genus of their own. My favourite forms are the large blue ones, but there are also pinks and mauves of varying degrees. So variable are they that to secure good forms one should see one's plant in flower. All these are forms of *Hepatica nobilis*, which was formerly known as *Anemone hepatica* or later *Hepatica tribola* from its three-lobed leaves. There is a slightly larger flowered species in Rumania and Hungary called *H. transsilvanica*, and the variety recommended and known as *angulosa* belongs to this species. They do, however, make good ground covers. The pale China blue forms are also attractive. The finest is known as 'Ballardii', a hybrid between the two species which was raised at Ballard's famous nursery at Colwall. It is a really lovely plant with flowers of the clearest powder-blue, and a clump lasts in flower for several weeks. The flowers are the size of a shilling, sometimes larger, and an old-established clump may carry a great number so that it is a wonderful sight. They are plants for the shadier part of the rock garden or the wild garden and even out of flower their trilobed leaves are decorative. In order to flower freely they need to become established, so once settled they should be left alone, the only treatment required being an occasional mulch with leaf mould. They are plants of the alpine woodland where they flower in May, but with us they will flower in February or March.

The periwinkles are also plants for the wild garden and many will be justifiably frightened of admitting them at all. They do, however, make good ground covers. I find the golden varigated one of the best variegated plants and a great asset in winter brightening up a dull corner, and by clipping off the long streamers it can be kept in its clumps. The main winter flowerer of the genus is *Vinca difformis*, and it will produce blossoms at intervals throughout the winter whenever there is any sunshine for encouragement, but the flowers are always considerably paler in their mauve than those of the common *Vinca major* and *V. minor*. Even these are so accommodating and their growth so vigorous that they are seldom cherished. They will cover dry or shaded banks where little else seems to flourish.

Of the violets there are legion, both in species and variety, but the majority flower later than our season of winter and early spring. One of my favourites is *V. septentrionalis*, which flowers normally in March, the flowers being large and white and delicately veined with mauve towards the centre.

The scented violets and their swollen and generally less sweet varieties, such as are more commonly sold in the streets, flower at intervals throughout the late winter and early spring months, especially if grown in a frame and well pampered with gross feeding and water in the summer. The best of the ordinary violets is probably still 'Princess of Wales' and of the Parma violets 'Duchesse de Parme'. No new varieties seem to have been produced recently.

HELLEBORES

Few gardeners seem to realise the range of colour or the variety of the hellebores. They are not gaudy or brilliant plants, but they will grow in shady places and a succession of flowers can be raised from December to April, after which they begin to look a little tarnished although the petals are very persistent and may still hang on for a month or two longer. Their flowers are long lived and have the merit of growing old gracefully.

The white Christmas rose *Helleborus niger*, named from the colour of its root, is the best known, but even it is not so common as it used to be. The large white flowers well repay a cloche to cover them and keep them clean from the mud and rain. There is a wild variety with larger flowers known as *H. niger macranthus* or in some books *H. niger altifolius*, but the leaves tend to overtop and partly hide the flowers although they give them some protection. An earlier form has been distinguished as *praecox* which may begin to flower well before Christmas, but unfortunately both of these are rare in cultivation. A named form with larger flowers than the type, called 'Potter's Wheel', is also now available and its seedlings are almost indistinguishable from the parent. Occasional flowers five inches across have been recorded. All the Christmas roses seem to do best in a good enriched soil such as that of the kitchen garden.

One of the largest and to my mind most exciting species is *H. corsicus*, whose home is Corsica, but its distribution also extends into Italy. The flowers are yellow-green, cup-shaped and borne in a loose head which often grows two feet or more high and carries a number of flowers. In spite of its greenish colour, it is, however, always a conspicuous plant, both from its foliage and its flowers. I well remember finding it in flower in January on the sides of the lanes leading up to the hill-top towns of the south-east coast of Italy – little castellated towns growing like fairy castles out of the tops of their hills. The yellow stamens and bright green carpels stood out vividly against the paler circle of the flower. The leaves are very sharply serrated and often bear a slight white bloom and so add a distinctive touch of their own to any flower decoration. It is very common in Corsica where it makes very large clumps often a yard or more across, while even in late May the flowers were still decorative. In English gardens it begins to show the buds in December and, depending on the season, these open between January and mid-March and continue in flower for a long time. As a foliage plant it is absolutely in the front rank throughout the year.

Close to *H. corsicus* botanically is *H. lividus* with even more decorative leaves and more jade-like flowers, but it is somewhat tender and lacks the vigour of *H. corsicus*. Some botanists now list *H. corsicus* as a subspecies of *H. lividus*, the older name, and this has the advantage of conserving the name *corsicus* as against the much lesser-known name of *H. argutifolius* by which it is sometimes called. There is also a group of hybrids between *H. lividus* and *H. corsicus* which were first recognised at Highdown and named *H.* x *sternii* after its owner the late Sir Frederick Stern. They are very variable, some verging more to *H. corsicus*, others towards *H. lividus*, but most are good garden plants flowering about February. Even more choice are the hybrids between *H. niger* and *H. corsicus* which are known under the group name *H.* x *nigricors*. The flowers are generally creamy-white and are larger and taller than those of *H. niger* but they usually are closer to that parent. Several have been raised recently but unfortunately they are still rare in cultivation.

In January, sometimes in late December, the earliest of the purple hellebores *H. atrorubens* will come into flower and it is a very handsome plant. The form usually found in gardens is not the same as the wild species of the same name but appears to be a clone of unknown origin, and since there is no other the name needs to be retained for the present. The flowers stand well up above the foliage, a foot or more. A number of species have been named and these grade imperceptibly into the large hybrid group of Lenten Roses which are surely among the best plants for enjoyment of winter flowers.

From the white and green hellebores we can grade our collection gradually through all the tones of pinks and purple to the deepest maroon of *H. colchicus* from northern Asia Minor, which is as dark as a 'Sultan' sweet pea. It is a vigorous plant and has many forms, some clean in colour, others flecked with greens and yellows. Like so many plants from Asia Minor it appreciates lime. It also appreciates a damper position than the other species. Those heavily spotted at the base derive from *H. guttatus* and have given us some of the best flowers in the group.

A collection of the forms of the so-called Lenten Roses, *H. orientalis*, will provide flowers over a long period from January to April, and they always look well in a mixed winter bowl, although they do not last nearly as long as they do out of doors. They vary enormously and forms should be chosen in flower or seed taken from a good collection. I like to choose those which tend to have horizontal flowers, and so look at one, rather than those with more pendulous flowers. I also like to keep my best whites separate and also the very dark forms, some of which have a smoky sheen on the outside. One of the darkest has been named 'Black Knight' but unfortunately it lacks vigour and is very rarely seen. There is also a pale yellow form which is very desirable but, alas, even rarer. Theirs is a quiet but mellow beauty.

All hellebores take some time to become established after

63

moving or division and so this operation should not be done too frequently. The late Bertram Anderson, a great authority on the genus, recommended dividing the clumps in August and splitting them up into single crowns. I have, however, moved clumps and young plants quite successfully in March or April. Until established, they seldom flower well. The roots are mostly thick, fleshy and brittle, and like a good rich mixture with plenty of manure. Their placing in the winter garden is sometimes rather difficult, but since they are to remain some time in position, it is worth some attention. Against a yew hedge, provided the sunlight reaches them directly, they will look well, or one can try and back them with some brighter flowers of their own hue such as daphnes. Probably hamamelis would be too strong. They also mingle well with snowdrops and the dwarf blue anemones. Hellebores have been well esteemed in classical times for their supposed medicinal qualities.

We have two native species with green flowers, *H. foetidus* and *H. viridis*. The former is a very decorative foliage plant, nearly as fine as *H. corsicus*. The flower spikes are large with clusters of real green thimble-like flowers each edged with dark crimson. In some gardens it spreads very freely from seedlings. *H. viridis* is smaller and more delicate and the flowers are a more jade-like green, while its foliage disappears during the summer. Both flower in February and March.

Sir Arthur Hort, in his delightful book 'The Unconventional Garden', quotes Theophrastus on the method of gathering Hellebores:

One should, it is said, draw a circle round the Hellebore, and cut it standing towards the East and saying prayers, and one should look out for an eagle, both on the right and on the left; for there is danger to those that cut, if your eagle should come near, that they may die within the year.

PRIMULAS

My favourite early-flowering Primula is *P. edgeworthii*, long

Magnolia × *soulangiana*, an old specimen. (W. Abbing)

(*Above*) *Magnolia stellata* at Kew. (Reginald A. Malby & Co.)

(*Below*) *Magnolia campbellii* subsp. *mollicomata*, a lovely flower in a famous Cornish garden.

and probably better known under the name of *P. winteri*. It is indeed a winter or early spring flowerer, opening its delicate powder blue flowers in late February or early March. In form and size like an ordinary primrose with slighter, shorter stems, the flowers have a pale yellow eye, the lobes of the corolla being deeply indented and slightly fringed, framed by the most attractive leaves which are covered with a silvery-grey mealy powder, coming off at a touch. In spite of Farrer's remarks about the 'cruciferous rampageousness' of the plant, and the long time during which it has been introduced, *P. edgeworthii* is still an uncommon plant on the rock garden. Like most of the Petiolarid class of primulas it is sensitive over winter damp round its collar, and rough weather will destroy much of the silvery mealiness of the leaves. It grows well, however, in a vertical cleft in the rock-work where its roots can find a damp run and its crown is somewhat protected. It is also excellent for the alpine house. It is one of those rare plants where the leaves and flowers are in perfect harmony with each other, and as such well worth a special effort.

Primula winteri was not named after its winter flowering habits, in latinised English, as one might have feared at first glance, but after Mr Winter who was a Commissioner in Kumaon in the Himalayas and first introduced it in 1908. His description of his find, recorded in the R.H.S. Journal for 1923, is worth quoting since it conveys vividly the excitement to be derived from the discovery of such a fine plant:

Growing at the edge of the snow I saw a patch of blue looking lovely with the rising sun shining on it between the trunks of the trees, in delightful contrast with the white of the snow and its whitened leaves. It was a primrose with 20 or 30 blooms: at that elevation and with that clear atmosphere, really blue without that mauvish tint which it has chosen to assume in duller England. I realised it was more beautiful than any primrose I had ever seen.

Like so many of this group, it seems to grow better in the longer winters and cooler summers in Scotland than in the south of England where a really dry hot summer may kill it. Other beauties of the group are *P. whitei* (formerly known as *P. bhutanica*) and *P. sonchifolia*, the largest of all and one which needs to be kept very moist. Both of these have wonderful clear ice-blue flowers in very early spring.

Another modern favourite of the same class is *Primula scapigera;* the leaves, however, haven't the same mealiness and the flowers are not a very intense shade of pink – in fact, in my eyes the whole plant lacks the extreme distinction of *P. edgeworthii.* It is probably, however, easier to grow.

For a bog or water edge there are few plants more brilliant than *Primula rosea.* Its pink flowers often appear during March and are so violent, almost harsh in their pinkness that careful placing is necessary. I know of no flower that carries the quality of pinkness to a greater extreme. It is real pink too, not in any way scarlet or crimson or purple. The finest form is known as 'Delight'. The flowers are borne in a loose globose head, the first opening almost in the crown of the plant, and then emerging upwards as the stem elongates. Again, provided one has a damp and sunny situation there is no difficulty over its growth, and it will often seed itself. Without the moisture it seldom seems to maintain and establish itself. It is not a plant for the formal garden, yet it is well set off by grey stone if a place can be found between the water and the stones. It combines well with the bright yellow skunk cabbage, *Lysichitum americanum,* which flowers equally early and before its vast leaves are developed. It looks like a much larger and much more brilliant yellow aroid of the Lords and Ladies type and again will only do well in a moist place.

P. clarkei is also a charming little pink beauty for the alpine house or the very special spot in the rock garden. It belongs however to a different section and is usually considered easier to grow than members of the Petiolarid section. The flowers are smaller and a little less intense in colour than those of *P. rosea.*

A plant that should present no trouble in cultivation is *Primula* 'Wanda,' a form of primrose, which flowers very early in the year; often a few flowers appear in January during a warm spell. The earliest are almost sessile, nestling into the crown of the plant; they are deep reddish-purple in colour, glowing like a glass of wine held up to the light while the plants are generally covered with flowers. The later flowers are larger and longer stalked. A good patch will attract the eye irresistibly from a distance and hold it until one reaches the plants. There is no looking away. Surely that is a desirable plant? No alpine house is needed to rear it, no fortune to buy it and no great skill to propagate or grow it. It is already widely spread, and should be in every garden.

The common primrose needs no eulogies from me. It is a worthy plant for all gardens, great or small. I would like to see cultivated again too some of the attractive coloured varieties and double forms at which our ancestors undoubtedly excelled us. 'Madame de Pompadour' was a delightful old double primrose like deep crimson velvet, while among the old polyanthus we find such fascinating names as 'Jack-a-napes', a creamy-yellow variety, 'Pantaloons' and 'Galligaskins', surely worth growing for their names alone, although I cannot tell you where to find them at present.

The butter-yellow polyanthus 'Barrowby Gem' is also one of the finest and largest in flower and will very often bloom during any mild spells between January and March.

Another plant for the careful connoisseur is *Primula allionii* whose pink flower-covered tussocks always attract attention at the early shows of the year. It is a plant of the Maritime Alps and very variable in colour, so one should buy it in flower if possible. Like many primulas, it is very intolerant of any soggy conditions, and immaculate drainage and care over a long period seem to be the secret of those wonderful specimens covered with great pink, almost sessile flowers, jostling each other for space to open. It does well in the alpine house, although it may sometimes be established outside in a crevice in a vertical rock face. It is a plant of the limestone.

PULMONARIAS AND LITHOSPERMUMS

Real strong gentian blues are rare in winter, but there is a form of *Pulmonaria*, the lungwort, which possesses that colour, and which should be cultivated much more frequently for it is an easy plant, spreading freely, yet without the coarseness that many of this genus are inclined to display. The form I refer to has the ponderous name of *Pulmonaria angustifolia azurea* and the best garden form is that known as 'Mawson's Blue.' The leaves, incidentally, are not particularly narrow.

The foliage of this form is unspotted as in the common lungwort and while ample in amount, it mostly develops later than the flowers and so does not swamp them. These are borne on stems a foot or so high and each stem ends in a bunch of tubular flowers of the richest, deepest blue. It has not the rich satin gloss of the gentian, but it certainly has the colour, a deep prussian-indigo flower, lightening slightly as the flower ages. Usually the plants begin to flower towards the end of February and continue throughout March. In a warmer year they will begin earlier. They can be propagated easily by division and a great patch of them overhanging a rock will prove an attraction which will hold the eye, even from a distance.

The flowers are slightly pendulous and are seen best either at eye level or slightly above, so the lungworts should be planted, if possible, near the top of the rock garden.

Pulmonarias are not particular over position; they will grow in shade and like leaf mould. In fact they are thoroughly adaptable plants. The forms are very variable. Some have a considerable amount of pink on the outside of the bud, others have larger and coarser leaves. It is important to pick out a really good all blue form when establishing one's colony. As well as the rock garden it is adapted to the front of the border or the edge of the woodland where in an open space it will spread widely and flower regularly every year.

There are also pink pulmonarias and probably the best is *P. rubra*, from Transylvania, unfortunately still an uncommon plant. The flowers often open as early as January, the foliage is unspotted and in the best forms the flowers are a warm and soft red, and do not follow the pulmonaria habit of turning a rather dirty purplish-red. The pulmonarias mingle well with the dwarf narcissi and in European woods sometimes the association is found thus. They seem to do best if divided rather frequently – every second or third year – rather than if left strictly alone for many years.

Recently a white lungwort has been offered under the name 'White Wings' and this should make a useful addition to the range.

The lithospermums are better known as spring and summer flowers although the common 'Heavenly Blue' will often linger through the winter months with an occasional flower during mild periods. My winter species, however, is *L. rosmarinifolium*, which has flowers as blue and as brilliant as the 'Heavenly Blue'. It is a more erect growing plant, and in really favourable situations will even make a small shrub, two to three feet high and covered with the strongest of blue flowers, opening from pink-tinged buds. The leaves are rich deep green and narrow, slightly inrolled like rosemary leaves. Unfortunately it is not quite so hardy as the ordinary 'Heavenly Blue' and can only be recommended for planting out doors in the southern and western counties. It does not require heat or excessive cultivation and will do well planted out in a bed of a cool unheated house, and used to be seen to perfection in the first greenhouse at Wisley, cascading over a rock before the range was moved to the Battleston Hill site. It will also do well in a pot on a window ledge and can be plunged out of doors during the summer, preferably in not too dry or exposed a position. It propagates freely, albeit rather slowly, from cuttings and it is worth trying to establish a few out of doors in the home counties in sheltered positions. They will probably survive until a specially hard winter tests our more delicate plants.

This winter species is a native of southern Italy and the neighbouring islands, particularly Capri where it grows on limestone rocks. In this country it flowers from the middle of November onwards till the end of March.

SAXIFRAGES

The early-flowering saxifrages are innumerable, both in species and still further in variety; so that here I can only attempt a very brief review of a few favourites. Everyone admires and covets the magnificently grown pans of saxifrages covered with flower that one sees at the spring shows. One hopes to do likewise in a year. These pans, however, are the result of many years' care and labour, never giving too much water in winter, never letting them get too dry in summer.

Many of these encrusted saxifrages can, however, be grown successfully on the open rock garden but it is necessary to prepare special positions for them. The silvery cushion class called 'Kabschia' are the finest and they are worth taking some trouble to grow well. They require a kind of scree or other open gritty mixture through which the water can drain away quickly during the winter. They are mostly plants of the Dolomites and like limestone chips or rocks or mortar rubble or all three combined. They are very intolerant of damp and soggy surroundings during winter and an open position away from trees suits them best. On the other hand, they do not want to be baked too much in summer and then like plenty of moisture flowing past their roots. Some keen gardeners have constructed artificial screes and so-called moraines with a system of underground watering from pipes pierced with holes, and this seems to have suited these saxifrages as well as other difficult alpines from the higher Alps. They are also among the finest plants for the alpine house, the scree frame or the more humble sink, and with such low-flowering plants it is a great advantage to have them raised to waist level. A glass over them in the latter half of winter is also very helpful in keeping off slugs and in protecting the flowers from being battered and spoilt by rain and mud.

Some of the finest are varieties of *Saxifraga burseriana* which has white flowers borne singly on reddish stems two or three inches high. The foliage is silvery like a little stiff pin-cushion. Several larger flowered varieties have been bred with flowers up to half an inch or even more in diameter. Notable among these are 'Gloria' with snow-white flowers and very red stems, 'His Majesty' with white flowers slightly flushed pink, 'Sulphurea' and 'Valerie Finnis' with soft citron-yellow flowers.

Two other rather similar hybrids should be mentioned here, though they have been derived from *S. aretioides* rather than *S. burseriana*. These are S. 'Boydii' and S. 'Faldonside', both with silvery-grey foliage and large soft flowers. 'Faldonside' is perhaps the easier plant of the two to grow. There is also a fine white variety of S. 'Boydii'. All these were raised by Mr Boyd in Scotland.

Another very early-flowering hybrid is 'Kellereri' which has silvery rosettes of rather long encrusted leaves and soft pink flowers. In some years it will start flowering in January. 'Irvingii' is also very early and free-flowering. The flowers are lilac-pink and it is quite dwarf.

Another of my favourites is *S. grisebachii* and this is also a very early flowerer. In February the silvery rosettes become humped up in the centre and from this hump the flowering shoot, often nine inches in height, arises, in this case bearing small flowers. Its wonderful character, however, is the thick purplish-crimson glandular hairs which cover the stem, the bases of the leaves and the large calyces and short red bracts. This gives a royal velvet appearance to the plant from the time the flowering spike first appears to the opening of the flowers, and this rich glowing colour is well displayed by the silvery leaves, although there is always something a little artificial about these plants. However, in a mixed alpine house they are among the plants to which one's eye is always drawn first. One cannot ignore them. The finest form is the 'Wisley Variety'.

Even earlier to flower and in many places easier to grow on

the open rock garden is *S. apiculata,* which has several rather
smaller pale lemon flowers bunched together on a three-inch
stem. It cannot be considered as such a distinguished plant as
some of the others mentioned but it is a better doer without
protection and will quickly make a large mat, flowering
regularly each year.

All over the Alps one finds *Saxifraga oppositifolia* cascading
over the rocks and screes in high places, making great splashes
and drifts of rich purple with myriads of little cups. It is even
a native of a few of the mountains of this country and in its
wild state it encourages one to regard it as one of the most
desirable of saxifrages; but somehow in only a very few rock
gardens does it become established, although it is more often
seen growing successfully in large pans in the alpine house.
Undoubtedly it wants to be kept dry during the winter, and in
the summer to have lots of water draining quickly through an
open mixture of shale and chips and sandstone. One of the
best forms is the 'Wetterhorn' variety which is a very rich dark
purple, almost ruby-red in colour. Even more jewel-like is
the little red ruby *S. retusa,* but it is rather a shy flowering plant
in England. The flowers are small but they seem to glow with a
wonderful intensity and sometimes in the Alps one finds a mat
of it covered with flower, an unforgettable sight.

S. fortunei from China and Japan is quite a different kind of
plant which really flowers in late autumn but is still frequently
in flower towards the end of November or early December
provided there has been no severe frost. The leaves are large,
slightly fleshy and dark crimson underneath, while the flowers
form white plumes a foot or more high and are very decorative
on the rock garden or at the edge of the shrubbery when there
is little else in flower. The flowers are irregular with the lower
petal much longer than the others.

Trees and Shrubs

CAMELLIAS

Camellias range from the most delightful early-flowering species with flowers like apple blossom or wild roses to some of the most sumptuous and superlative flowers of all our gardens. Among these are the varieties of *Camellia japonica* and *Camellia reticulata* which often measure six inches or more in diameter. It is of the smaller flowered species and varieties that I wish to speak first, because it is only in the last thirty years that their comparative hardiness has been proved and that stock has become more generally available. They have also been the parents of several very fine hybrids, and with the great popularity of camellias at present and the spate of newer hybrids that has occurred in recent years the selection is now very wide, but there are still probably great possibilities. In this section we will deal with their growing outside, and in the chapter on the Cool Greenhouse with those which show their flowers better under some protection although as plants they may be hardy enough. The ideal site is probably in an open woodland but they do not flower so well in shade and they can stand almost full sun. It is quite unnecessary to confine them to a north-facing wall. Like rhododendrons, though, they must have acid conditions in the soil and will not stand any lime.

The earliest species to flower is *Camellia sasanqua*, which in a favourable season may start in November and continue throughout mild spells for several months. The flowers of the type are white and single, but there are several garden varieties which have larger flowers with more pink colour in them. In form the flowers are about the size and colour of a wild dog rose and although they haven't quite the same frail charm, being stiffer and waxier, they have no thorns and some of the natural pose and dignity which one associates with camellias. The

73

best variety for this country is 'Narumi-gata' which has quite large creamy-white flowers, shaded pink towards the margins, and quite a strong scent. It seems to be the most reliable for flowering, but there are some others such as 'Briar Rose', a soft clear pink, and 'Hiryu', a deep crimson-red double from Japan. In England, though, the Sasanqua camellias do not flower with the same freedom as they do in warmer areas such as California. They should be given a warm sunny position.

In late February and March *Camellia saluenensis* and the fine hybrids derived from it will start flowering. This is one of George Forrest's most valuable introductions. The leaves are glossy and evergreen, slightly serrated, while the flowers are soft pink like a dog rose with centres full of yellow stamens. This is a rather loose lanky growing shrub, but if it is carefully pruned when young it should form a decent specimen. Two most magnificent hybrids were raised at Caerhays in Cornwall by the late Mr J. C. Williams by crossing *C. saluenensis* with a single pink form of *C. japonica* and formed the types of the great group known as *C. x williamsii*. These are 'J.C. Williams' and 'Mary Christian', the second being the deeper pink in colour. They are some of the freest flowering of all camellias and surpass most forms of *saluenensis*. The flowers are single, up to three inches in diameter and the centre is full of a mop of golden-yellow stamens. Even quite small plants seem to flower freely, and they are now becoming much more widely known and grown, for they are some of the best garden plants introduced this century. Many others have been raised since then. Usually the earliest to flower is 'November Pink' which can live up to its name. More recent introductions in this group have come from New Zealand and I particularly like 'Anticipation' and 'Grand Jury' – both clear pinks with a looser habit than in most of the others. However, there are few plants to surpass in quantity of flower or in general display 'Donation' raised at Borde Hill, a famous Sussex garden. Its season of flowering is a very long one. The flowers are semi-double like paeonies, a beautiful bright pink and large – up to four or even five inches across. One of the great advantages of these *williamsii* hybrids is that they drop their dying flowers, while in the *japonica* varieties these need to be removed by hand.

Another early-flowering hybrid which is worth growing is 'Cornish Snow', a cross between the small-flowered *C. cuspidata* and *C. saluenensis*. The flowers are under two inches across but they are so numerous that it lives up to its name.

Like paeonies and cherries, we associate camellias with the wonderful painting of China and I think that the queen of them all in this respect is *Camellia reticulata*, introduced to this country from the gardens of China in 1820 and first flowered in Kent in 1826. During the last century some gigantic plants, some with hundreds of flowers, were grown in conservatories where they are superb, and in the Greenhouse chapter we discuss some of the varieties and newer hybrids. The cultivated plants in China were all the semi-double and double varieties, and it is the semi-double form which is regarded by the horticultural trade as *C. reticulata*. It is an unusually beautiful plant, evergreen, with large dark leaves, dull on the upper surface, and with the venation clearly visible. All camellias are rather slow growers, especially when young, but in a favourable situation *C. reticulata* will grow into a small tree ten or fifteen feet high. The flowers are deep crimson-pink, glistening, rich and luscious, florally juicy as is a ripe peach. It is not a tight, compact flower, yet in the semi-double form it does not seem untidy. I have seen reports that the flowers are sometimes as much as nine inches across. This size is rare, but six inches is quite common.

Only in 1912 did George Forrest, one of the greatest of our plant collectors, find the wild single form of *C. reticulata*, although the semi-double form had been known for a hundred years. He found it growing in scrub, thickets and open pine forest, between six and eight thousand feet around Tengyueh in western Yunnan. In 1932 it flowered at Caerhays in Cornwall, J. C. Williams's famous garden, and a plate was prepared of it for the Botanical Magazine. It appears to be about as hardy as the semi-double form or perhaps slightly more hardy.

75

The semi-double form can be grown quite successfully out of doors in the south-western and similarly mild counties and I have seen some fine ones in Sussex gardens. It is more often placed against a north or east wall than against a south wall, so that the flower-buds are not encouraged to open too early in the year. In this position they do not receive early morning sun after a frost, but have time to thaw gradually. The late Lord Aberconway in the report of the Royal Horticultural Society shrub conference, however, said that on a south wall 'it grows much more closely and flowers to profusion' and I agree.

To most gardeners, however, 'camellia' implies the varieties of *C. japonica*, and in most seasons these will begin to flower outside before early March and go on through April. The plants of *C. japonica* in the old wild garden at Wisley and in many other gardens must be between twenty and thirty feet high, and they are covered with flowers each spring, some crimson and some white or pink. Some of the flowers may be destroyed by frost, but more nearly always come. They are a magnificent sight. Camellias like a position with a rather moist, acid, peaty soil, not water-logged, but with some underground moisture. They are generally grown in semi-shade if in the open, or against north or east walls. They should be protected as far as possible against wind and early morning sun.

The varieties of *Camellia japonica* are innumerable. The colour of the flower also varies with soil and position, and can even be varied from year to year as the acidity is varied. Deeper tints are produced in soils as acid as pH. 4 or lower. This is the optimum with plenty of sunshine. Lighter tints and less vigorous growth are produced on neutral soils. For outside I prefer the single and semi-double varieties to the completely double ones, and among these the old stalwarts 'Lady Clare', semi-double and deep clear pink, and 'Adolphe Audusson', a very deep crimson almost blood-red, are still among the best. These almost equal *C. reticulata* in size and charm. Of the lighter coloured forms, I recommend 'Magnoliaeflora'. The flowers are not so large as in the other varieties mentioned, but they are very perfectly formed, white just tinted with a faint warmth of pink. 'Peach Blossom' is one of the best varieties and is a slight but definite improvement on the type. 'White Swan' is a magnificent white single variety, glistening and snowy, very early and free-flowering and with a fine mass of yellow stamens in the centre of the flower; but I also like the single whites 'Alba Simplex' and 'Devonia', and the very early 'Nobilissima' which has almost double white flowers shading to pale yellow in the centre. 'Jupiter' is an excellent single red of great vigour. When Robert Fortune was sent to China by the Horticultural Society in 1843 he was specially charged among other things to enquire for paeonies with blue flowers and camellias with yellow flowers. Neither has ever been found, and the Secretary of the society added to the request the words 'the existence of which is doubtful'. At that time the interest in camellias was intense, but it has become so again, both on this and the other side of the Atlantic.

It has also been proved in recent years that camellias are very readily propagated from cuttings taken at the correct season, which is generally about July. The only difficult species is *C. reticulata*. Most camellias are now grown on their own roots rather than as grafted plants.

The genus *Camellia* was named by Linnaeus after a Jesuit priest, Joseph Kamel, whose latinised name was Camellus. He travelled in Asia towards the end of the seventeenth century and then settled in the Philippine Islands where he wrote an account of the plants. He can hardly have known how great would be his memorial.

CHERRIES, ALMONDS, PEACHES, APRICOTS AND PLUMS

All these sound very luscious in winter but it is here the flowers rather than the fruit which we will discuss and we should say right away that practically none of the varieties we shall mention produces very useful fruit. All these trees belong to the genus *Prunus*.

The most valuable winter-flowering cherry carries the rather cumbersome name of *Prunus subhirtella* var. *autumnalis* but nevertheless it is a plant which is worth a place in every garden. It makes a large twiggy bush or small tree and has the delightful habit of producing flowers in spasms throughout the warm intervals of the winter, generally finishing up with a mass of bloom covering the tree in early March. In some years the trees are in full bloom in November. The flowers are small but make up for their size by their numbers. The normal variety has white flowers, but in the variety 'Rosea', which I prefer, they are pink in bud opening to a pale blush pink and have the delicate pose and slight petaloid frills of a ballet dancer in the 'Swan Lake', though without their austere whiteness. Curiously, the early flowers are almost sessile on the bare twigs but as the season gets later the stalks of the flowers get larger until the flowers are quite pendulous. Unlike most cherries, the young twigs can be cut for the house when in bud without apparently harming the tree and this will keep it more compact. For winter flowers it is important to choose the variety *autumnalis*, but the normal species is also a valuable plant for flowering in the latter half of March or early April, while the weeping variety *pendula* 'Rosea' is particularly valuable when placed over a rock or when shaped as an umbrella. The flowers are pale pink and cascade down in plentiful showers. 'Fukubana' has even deeper pink flowers and is the strongest in colour of this group of cherries.

Our next cherry is *Prunus conradinae* and this is also a plant which should be very much more widely grown than it is. The flowers are slightly larger than those of *Prunus subhirtella*, pale pink in bud, opening almost white, single in the species but semi-double in the variety *semi-plena* which is the one that I would recommend. Flowering in early March before the leaves are out, it rarely fails to cover itself with blossom. The buds seem to be very resistant to frost, and only an air frost when it is actually in flower or first opening will blacken the flowers. It makes a large bush or, if grown as a standard, a small tree rather of the shape and form of a hazel. Both the species mentioned are eminently suitable for the small garden where space is restricted, since they do not grow at the rate or attain the size of either the double white cherry or the pink 'Kanzan', so often found in diminutive front gardens. Also excellent for such situations is the fastigiate 'Amano-gawa' cherry which will grow like a Lombardy poplar and is covered with pink flowers, but it is a much later flowering variety and hardly comes into the terms of reference for this book.

Some of the forms of the Fuji cherry *P. incisa* will also flower early and two forms have been named, 'February Pink' and 'Praecox'. These make small trees with numerous small flowers either white with pink buds or pale blush-pink. Some of them also have fine scarlet autumn colouring in the foliage which gives them a second period of interest, but the best for this feature is *P. sargentii* which in a favourable season will also flower in March. I regard this as one of the best trees for every small garden. Captain Collingwood Ingram, our greatest authority on cherries, has also raised two very good small cherries, 'Kursar' and 'Okame', which flower very early. 'Okame' has masses of small pink flowers with deeper pink buds often in February, since it has as one parent the tender crimson-flowered *P. campanulata* which flowers then with its leaves but is too tender outside in this country. This tenderness, however, has not been inherited and so 'Okame' is one of our most valuable and beautiful early cherries. Unfortunately, though, it is very susceptible to bird damage to the buds. 'Kursar' flowers a little later and is a *sargentii* hybrid, but it has deeper pink flowers than 'Okame' and seems an equally valuable tree.

The almonds are well known and need no description from me. They are one of the few examples of really valuable plants which are deservedly popular and widely planted. Probably the best variety is 'Pollardii' which flowers slightly earlier than the type and whose flowers are slightly larger and deeper pink. This fine almond originated in Australia with a Mr Pollard and was first called Pollard's Peach. Its parentage is

79

not known with certainty but it is thought to be a hybrid between an almond and the Pen-too peach. It is certainly a very fine plant and seems vigorous enough although some say it is not quite so vigorous as the type.

Almonds need careful placing. Their flowers show up well against a dark background of evergreens or against a blue sky. On the other hand they lose much of their character against an amorphous shrubby background. It is also well, I think, to plant them where the sun can reach their roots and provide first a little warmth to the soil around them. This seems to apply even though the crowns may be in full sun. All Prunus grow well on chalk, but it is not a necessity and they are probably one of the most adaptable of all genera over soil and cultivation and provide a wonderful investment for any garden. All almonds are very susceptible to bird damage to the buds especially in the open country and for this reason some gardeners have given up growing them. A small tree can be protected to some degree by festooning it with cotton. Curiously they seem to flower better in towns and near main roads where there is more disturbance to the birds.

There is also a most attractive dwarf almond which forms a spreading shrub, suckering freely and growing no more than two feet in height. I know one garden where there is a large patch of it which is a mass of bloom early in March every year. The best form is *Prunus tenella* 'Gessleriana' which has larger pink flowers than the type. Very similar is 'Fire Hill' which is perhaps a little more bush-like. No attempt should be made to restrict this plant to any definite form, but it should be left alone to ramble freely in a sunny position. It is sometimes called the dwarf Russian Almond. As in Mr Bowles's garden, it may be underplanted with bulbs such as muscaris and crocuses which will live well and undisturbed among its dwarf forest of stems and present a fine picture of natural gardening, the most satisfactory form of gardening of all when it is successful.

The best of the early peaches is *Prunus davidiana* named after that wonderful old French missionary Père David, one of the

The stylosa iris. *I ungui-cularis*, by many consid-ered the finest winter-flowering plant. (H. Smith)

Hamamelis mollis 'Pallida' which usually flowers in January.

Magnolia campbellii. Some consider this the most magnificent of all flowering trees. (J. E. Downward)

finest of that group of indefatigable French missionary collectors who worked in China during the last century. *P. davidiana* is the earliest peach to flower, often producing its pink blossoms in February. There is also an excellent white-flowered variety which is generally a little earlier than the pink form. The flowers are rather almond-like in form, single and up to an inch in diameter, and are produced over the full length of the previous year's growth, albeit sometimes a bit spasmodically during mild spells. This plant requires careful placing in the winter garden and generally shows best when the flowers are seen against a background of dark evergreens.

It is probably a contradiction in terms to suggest that any plant is artificial looking, yet the flowers of *Prunus triloba* immediately suggest to me posies of artificial tissue paper flowers or even sugar decorations on a fancy cake. Undoubtedly it should be the other way round, and *P. triloba* should be grown much more widely than it is. The flowers are a real pink, slightly deeper than those of the almond, double and borne very freely along the bare branches. Flowering in mid-March to early April, it thrives best against a wall in the counties round London, but this is not necessary along the south coast or in the west. A red wall will kill the pink of the flowers but a white wall is a perfect background. It also makes an excellent plant for bringing on in a cool conservatory in tubs or large pots, and many will remember the lovely display of it in the temperate house at Kew together with forsythias and almonds in tubs flanking the centre path down the vast house, backed by the lovely grey pendulous *Cupressus cashmeriana* and the tree ferns and camellias. If you have never seen this, I strongly recommend you to visit Kew in March and walk right up the gardens to the temperate house. *Prunus triloba* has always been a great favourite in Chinese gardens and was one of the earliest plants to be introduced from China. Considering the long time it has been grown in this country it is surprisingly, and I think undeservedly, rare in English gardens. The flowers are generally a good inch in diameter with rounded overlapping petals and a kind of posy centre. It should be pruned hard directly after flowering since it is on the long shoots of the previous season's growth that the flowers are produced. The desirable double form is described in catalogues as *flore-pleno* and this is one of the few plants where I recommend the double in preference to the single form.

The true peaches are as beautiful in flower as they are luscious in fruit, and for those who have no wall space the growing of bush peaches is now finding increasing favour, especially if they can be planted on a high part of the garden where the frost will drain away downhill from them. Of the decorative double peaches the form 'Russell's Red' is very desirable, being a magnificent deep crimson in colour and double in flower. Two more recent hybrids which I can recommend are 'Aurora' with double rose-pink flowers and 'Iceberg' with semi-double white ones. They are lovely underplanted with chionodoxas or grape hyacinths. All these peaches seem to suffer badly from leaf curl if they are unattended and will well repay being included in the spraying programme given to the fruit trees.

The apricots are also little grown in English gardens: the Japanese apricot *Prunus mume* flowers early in the year, often as early as the almond, and the pale pink flowers are attractive against the rather dark wood. It is, however, somewhat more susceptible to frost than the almond and in the counties around and north of London does best when planted against a south wall. A very lovely deep pink double form from Japan is 'Beni-shi-don'.

Of the early-flowering plums the commonest is that known as *pissardii*. It is a plant that requires careful placing so that the very pale flowers are seen to the best advantage. It can be very lovely in March, especially when grown as a tall tree with the branches thinned slightly. I remember one which grew almost against the bedroom window of a house and was lit up each morning by the spring sun. The disadvantage of this plant is the thick mop of deep plum-coloured foliage which develops in the summer and seems to mingle so inharmoniously with the greens of the garden. In this respect I haven't yet managed to find the perfect situation for it. It is a tree of great vigour and seems to flower freely each year, requiring little attention, and so is deservedly popular for small suburban gardens. This is named after M. Pissart, a French gardener of the last century, and should more correctly be described as *pissartii*, though the name *pissardii* is securely established in most catalogues. Slightly pinker and probably better in most gardens is 'Blireana' which is thought to be a hybrid between *pissardii* and an apricot.

The ordinary Myrobalan plum *P. cerasifera* is also very early flowering and when allowed to grow freely makes a delightful tree covered in March with white flowers. Branches of it can be picked for the house and will last a few days before dropping. For the wild hedgerow the Myrobalan plum is excellent, but I do not recommend it for a hedge which has to be trimmed frequently. It also has the advantage of producing crops of small plums which are quite palatable to eat and are good for jam-making.

Of the main Japanese cherries few come into our category, but one of the best, *Prunus yedoensis*, will in a favourable year flower before the end of March. The flowers are white with just the palest pink tinge, freely produced in clusters, slightly double, and the plant is a good vigorous grower, quickly making a small tree. There are a number of specimens of this Prunus at Kew and they are a delight every spring.

Captain Collingwood Ingram also recommends 'Fudan Zakura', a Japanese cherry for winter flowering. The buds are pink and flowers white and single, opening in clusters on the bare stems during fine intervals from February onwards.

The ordinary blackthorn will also in favourable years come within our category and is nowhere seen to such advantage as against the stone walls of the Cotswold country. However, for wild hedgerows it might well be planted more frequently. It is always thick and impenetrable, the main characteristics of a good hedgerow plant.

DAPHNES

Daphne mezereum, often called just the 'Mezereon', is one of the oldest established and one of the very toughest and most fragrant and generally one of the best of our winter-flowering shrubs. Although a native of much of central Europe from Switzerland to Siberia and grown in this country for several centuries, it is surprising how rarely a large specimen is met. Daphne also seems to be one of those subjects which are more often found thriving in the good cottage garden than in the larger gardens of mansions. No certain reason can be given for this.

Nearly the size and not unlike the form of lilac bloom, the flowers are borne thickly along the upper lengths of the main shoots before the leaves appear. When the leaves do appear the young shoots grow away from the ends above the flowers. In colour the flowers vary, the best forms being a deep purple-crimson, the poorest a rather washy lilac. So it is important, if possible, to see one's daphne in flower or select seed from a good form. The seed is borne in bright red fleshy berries which are decorative in themselves. They ripen during the late summer and should be sown then. There is also a very beautiful white-flowered variety with yellow berries, which some say is even stronger smelling than the purple-red type. This, however, I would not like to promise. The best form of this is 'Bowles' White' which is erect in growth, more vigorous than the type and has tall spikes of ivory-white flowers. It seems to come fairly true from seed and I have seen plants five feet tall.

It is probable that in this country at any rate the 'Mezereon' is not generally a very long-lived plant and one very seldom sees old plants more than four feet in height and four feet through. Such a plant would be a most magnificent sight in the winter sunshine. Although in much of its native habitat a grower on limestone formations, it seems in England to grow equally well off the lime as on it. Probably one of its dislikes is getting too dry in summer and it definitely responds to generous cultivation, although bitterly resenting any attempt at moving. Daphnes should be put in their final position when quite young. In some gardens seedlings appear freely though they have never done this with us. I have often thought of planting a little bed devoted to daphnes by our front porch, where one could smell them as one went to work each winter morning. They have a long flowering season, often beginning in December and carrying on till the end of March, and like the hamamelis and the jasmine are wonderfully resistant to frost.

Gerard cultivated the 'Mezereon' as long ago as 1597 and writes that he received the seed from Poland, possibly through a trader of the Hanseatic League. He prescribes the berries as a cure for drunkenness, stating: 'Also if a drunkard do eat one grain or berry of this plant, he cannot be allowed to drink at that time, such will be the heat of his mouth and choking in the throat.'

These daphnes seem to combine well with other plants, appearing rather gaunt and leggy on their own, and seem to appreciate the root covering provided by one of the winter-flowering varieties of *Erica carnea*, many of which act as a fine foil to them.

There are also several other species of daphne which are worth planting in the winter garden and some of them are much beloved by plant connoisseurs, possibly partly because of their fickle habits of growth, partly because of their quiet and unblatant beauty. Some are especially plants for the rock garden, and *Daphne blagayana*, a species from the eastern Alps with recumbent stems and quite large terminal clusters of very sweet-smelling creamy flowers in March and April, is worth trying in every garden. This plant roots from the tips of the recumbent branches and seems especially to appreciate a stone placed over the branch to keep it in place. In some gardens it will ramble until it has made a large patch and the more blasé gardeners airily remark that they throw a stone at it whenever passing. Be this as it may, it definitely does appreciate help from stones in rooting from the trailing branches.

Less hardy in the home counties but still a good plant for gardens in the south and west is *Daphne odora*, a very fragrant species with flowers reddish-purple on the outside, produced densely in terminal heads. It may flower in midwinter but usually starts in February and may continue till the spring; but the display effect is somewhat masked by the fact that it is evergreen. It is also a native of China and Japan. Slightly the hardiest form is that with yellow edges to the leaves, 'Aureomarginata,' and it seems hardy enough in gardens around London in a sheltered sunny position. The flowers have a wonderful scent, a rival to any scent shop. Some old veterans survive but in general it does not appear to be a very long-lived plant.

Another evergreen species which flowers in February and March is *Daphne laureola* and its yellowish-green flowers have a curious charm, but they lack that supreme characteristic of the daphnes: the strong fragrant scent. It is a native plant and perhaps more suitable for woodland than garden planting. It is afflicted with the rather unhappy name of Spurge Laurel.

Daphne pontica is a better plant, also with green flowers and with good scent. It flowers usually towards the latter part of March but in a cold season may not open till April.

A close relation of the daphnes is *Edgeworthia papyrifera*, which has dense clusters of scented buff-yellow flowers which are tubular and covered towards the base with silky white hairs. This will make a bush four or five feet high, flowering in February or March, but unfortunately it is tender except in the milder counties, otherwise it would surely be much more widely grown.

HAMAMELIS

The hamamelis, or Witch Hazels, have always seemed to me rather unnatural flowers, nevertheless they have a very distinct attraction, and should be as widely grown as the winter jasmine. They present no greater difficulty as long as the soil is not limy.

The petals are narrow twisting strips which appear on the bare branches as little pieces of yellow tissue paper gathered together into a minute ragged posy at the base. There is no regular form to the flowers, they twist in all directions as a spindly Medusa's head. The finest species is *Hamamelis mollis* from China, whose flowers are probably the largest of the genus and a rich bright yellow which glows and gleams in the sun. All the hamamelis are rather difficult to place so that they can be seen to the best effect. They look well against a dark green background of yews provided that some sunlight reaches them directly and lights them up; that means they should be placed on the south or west side and not too close, so that their roots are not robbed by the yew roots. Alternatively, when they grow large, as they will in a few years, they look very well raised on a mound so that one sees them from below, outlined against a blue sky, that is on the days in winter when there is a blue sky. The top of a large rock garden would be a suitable place.

H. mollis becomes a large shrub or even a small tree, but the slightly later-flowering *H. japonica arborea* makes a larger tree and is probably the most vigorous of all. Often *H. mollis* will begin flowering by Christmas and continue for a month or more in flower. Only the very strongest frosts seem to damage it. It is good also for cutting and in the house gives off its spicy scent.

Then *H. japonica* and its forms *arborea* and *zuccariniana* follow in January and February. The flowers of *H. japonica arborea* are rather paler and smaller than those of *H. mollis* and each petal has a deep reddish calyx, which gives it a slightly warmer colouring than *H. mollis*. It is not nearly such a showy plant however, the flowers tending to be rather lost against the background unless it is very carefully placed. The variety *zuccariniana* is a more showy plant with petals of citron yellow, strong and bold in colour as a lemon.

The best of the lemon-yellows, however, and some think the finest witch hazel, is 'Pallida', which makes a large spreading shrub. It is probably a seedling of *H. mollis* and often starts to flower in late December. The flowers seem slightly larger than in the type and certainly show up much more strongly owing to their acrid lemon-yellow. Other good forms recently selected are 'Brevipetala' in which the flowers seem to have petals of a deeper orange closely aggregated in a bunch, although slightly shorter than in the type; 'Goldcrest' with deep golden-yellow flowers with stronger red colouring at the base; and 'Coombe Wood' which has a spreading habit and flowers slightly larger than in the type.

Hybrids between *H. japonica* and *H. mollis* have also been raised, many at the famous arboretum of the de Belders at Kalmthout. Some of these have ruby-red flowers and the best of them are probably 'Jelena' and 'Ruby Glow'. They are difficult to place, however, so that the flowers show up at their best, but they do have the great advantage of magnificent scarlet autumn foliage, the finest in the genus.

Probably the earliest witch hazel to flower is the North American species *H. virginiana* and it carries its little round seed heads and its flowers together, hence the curious name *Hamamelis*, derived from the Greek words 'hama' with and 'melon' fruit. The flowers are less showy than those of the other species and often begin to open before all the leaves have fallen in November. They are yellow in colour and rather thin and spidery. This hamamelis is used often as a stock on which to graft the choicer varieties. It is followed by *H. vernalis* in December and January, another North American species with yellow flowers but it is not nearly so distinctive a plant as *H. mollis*.

All the hamamelis should be planted in an open position where the sun can ripen their branches, and after warm summers they will often produce a fine display of autumn colouring; the leaves turning from yellow to a strong orange-red. They are about the size and form of the leaves of the laurel. The degree of colouring seems to vary very much with the season and the soil, but in some situations it can be very brilliant, nearly as fiery as the Parrotia. In a shady situation little autumn colour is developed.

HEATHERS

The Heath garden is a comparatively modern development in gardening; nevertheless it is a very satisfactory way of dealing with a small undulating piece of ground and if carefully planned there is probably no month in the year when there will not be some colour in it. Heathers are also very suitable for the large rock garden and for carpeting patches in the winter garden, providing a delightful foil to the daphnes, hamamelis and viburnums. There are few greens so rich and so bright in winter as that of *Erica arborea alpina* and it will provide a welcome background of height to the lower growing heathers in front, while in March, sometimes earlier, the shrubs will be covered with little white bells. Although I have seen great tree heathers often eighty feet high on the mountains of Equatorial Africa, in this country, or at any rate in the counties around London, one seldom sees specimens more than six or eight feet in height. The majority of our forms are derived from Spain and the Mediterranean countries, but they are not too tender to withstand our winters.

With a group of plants that flower throughout the year it is difficult to claim that the heather season begins at any one point. In October we shall find several varieties of the common ling *Calluna vulgaris* in flower. One of the best and most vigorous of these is 'H. E. Beale' with long sprays of double pink flowers. It is a most decorative plant and has a flowering season of mid-September till mid-November. I well remember the magnificent groups of this plant on the rock garden at Edinburgh Botanic Garden. Equally fine, and some even think superior, is 'Peter Sparkes' which also has double flowers of a good shell-pink. 'Else Purnell' and 'J. H. Hamilton' are two other favourites with pink flowers. There is also a good deep crimson variety of the common ling called 'Alportii', and two white-flowering varieties, 'Hammondii' flowering in September and October and 'Serlei' flowering a little later in the year.

A more recent development which is becoming very popular for the winter garden is heathers where the colour is in the foliage rather than in the flowers and so it lasts for a long time. 'Golden Feather' has deep golden-yellow foliage changing to a soft orange in winter while 'Gold Haze' is even brighter and has white flowers. Perhaps the most striking of these, though, is 'Blazeaway' whose foliage becomes in winter a bright orange-red, but it does make a rather obtrusive note among the soft colours of the heather garden.

The heather season is continued from December till March by varieties of *Erica carnea*, which is also one of the very few heathers which is tolerant of lime in the soil. For this reason its range of suitability for English gardens is very wide. It is absolutely hardy, withstanding the hardest frosts and snow, and if the different varieties are planted it has a long season of flowering from December till April. I have sometimes seen Christmas dinner tables decorated most effectively with *E. carnea*. The earliest varieties to flower are generally 'Gracilis' with bright pink flowers and 'King George' with deep crimson flowers followed by 'Winter Beauty' with deep pink flowers about Christmas. It is, however, very close to 'King George'. The type species has rather lighter rosy-red flowers. They are bottle shaped like the other ericas and all the plants are very free-flowering, often forming a regular carpet of colour six inches or more in height. The best of the later flowering varieties are 'Vivellii' with real deep crimson flowers, and 'Springwood White', the flowers of which are a really good clean white, contrasting well with the fresh green of the younger foliage. 'Springwood Pink' is equally good and both are very vigorous. They can be planted a foot or more apart and should close up in the second year.

Erica darleyensis is a very useful hybrid between *E. carnea* and *E. mediterranea*. It grows rather taller than *E. carnea*, often making eighteen inches in height and covering itself with spikes of pinkish-purple flowers, not so rich in colour as those of 'Vivellii' but still a cheering sight in midwinter. It is well worth planting in a big patch and probably from such a patch there will always be some flowers between November and March.

Of the taller growing heaths we have already mentioned *E. arborea* and its variety *alpina*. The other two worth growing are *E. lusitanica* sometimes called *E. codonodes*, the Portugal Heath, and *E. australis*. These are both somewhat more tender than *E. arborea alpina*, but still well worth trying in a sheltered place in the south and south-west and even in the counties around London. *E. lusitanica* flowers in February and March before *E. arborea alpina* and a finely developed specimen up to ten feet may sometimes bear thousands of the little white bell-shaped flowers hanging among the fresh green needle foliage. When coming out the flowers have a distinct rosy hue from the outside of the unopened buds. All these tree heaths are delicately fragrant in flower. *E. australis* and its forms flower rather later, generally beginning towards the end of March and continuing through April. They also reach ten feet or more in favoured situations and are covered with rosy-purple flowers. There is an excellent white-flowered variety called 'Mr Robert', named after the son of the late Charles Williams of Caerhays in Cornwall. He found it during a visit to Spain. These tree heaths can be trimmed a little by pruning the flowering shoots back slightly immediately they have finished flowering and this will encourage a more bushy habit.

All these heaths are easily propagated from division, from cuttings, or from layering and will grow freely without any very extensive preparations, particularly on a sandy-peaty soil. They do less well on the heavier clay soils where it is well worth mixing in some peat and coarse sand. A little summer moistness at the roots will also be appreciated, but is not essential. All the heathers should be planted if possible in large patches or drifts as small plants by themselves do not make sufficient show. If small plants are placed nine inches or so apart they will quickly grow together and form a soil covering which will require very little weeding or further attention. A heather garden is one of the most labour-saving kinds of gardening.

All these heathers associate well with conifers such as the upright grey *Juniperus hibernica* and also with pines and silver birches in the background. They do not associate well with formal or herbaceous bedding.

MAGNOLIAS

It is difficult to resist writing about such a magnificent genus and its finest members come into our category, flowering in late February and March. I refer to the group which includes *Magnolia campbellii* and *M. sargentiana* although its best known representative, *M. denudata* (*conspicua*) the Yulan, is rather an April than a March plant. It depends so much on the season. A warm March will bring a number of fine magnolias into flower while a very late season may delay them until the middle of April. The kind of day that suggests spring, however, at the end of March or early in April, is the day to go down to Kew and look at the magnolias. They are very fine there, not only near the front gate but also over on the far side of the garden.

The earliest of the smaller white-flowered species is *M. stellata* and this is a plant which should be in every garden, flowering abundantly and beginning to do so when the plant is quite small. It is also a more dwarf and compact grower than many of the *denudata* group and there are few specimens in this country even now over fifteen feet in height, although it has been grown for more than fifty years. The buds are furry and well protected and do not burst until a warm spell comes along. The flowers have not the perfect cup-shaped form of the Yulan and the petals are inclined to straggle and fall about the place as they go over. However, the flowers generally so cover the bush that their individual form is masked by the mass, and the general effect is one of a fine sprinkling of snow covering the bush and gleaming in the sun. Sometimes these magnolias are grown very effectively as an umbrella-shaped thicket with four or five plants well spaced. In this way a certain form is given to a plant which tends otherwise to be rather shapeless. There is also a good variety, *rosea*, with pale blush-pink flowers maturing to white.

A range of hybrids has been raised between *M. kobus*, a white-flowering species, and *M. stellata* or *M. stellata rosea*. The later cross has given us 'Leonard Messel', a very pretty and free-flowering plant usually well covered even on quite young bushes. In time it will make a small tree. The flowers are a delicate pink, slightly verging on lilac-pink, but they look very pretty in an open woodland and seem a little larger than those of *M. stellata*. The best white-flowering magnolia of this cross was raised in America at the Arnold Arboretum and has been named *M. x loebneri* 'Merrill' after the great American botanist. It is one of the most vigorous and free-flowering of all the magnolias, making a splendid effect in late March or early April, or possibly earlier in gardens in the milder areas. The flowers are also scented.

About the same season come two other magnolias with masses of white strap-shaped flowers, but when fully grown they can make a great effect. They are *M. salicifolia* and *M. kobus*. These are rather similar in flower but can be distinguished by the leaves; those of *M. kobus* are much broader. Both species are fastigiate in form reaching tree dimensions in time. The flowers are abundantly produced when the plants are mature and in both species are several inches in diameter, the petals, however, falling rather loosely about as in *M. stellata* rather than forming the perfect cup shape of the Yulan. In both these species the flowers are produced before the leaves, generally towards the end of March or early April depending on the season and locality. Mr Williams of Caerhays in Cornwall wrote, however, that *M. kobus* gave more bloom there than any other magnolia. Such a plant makes up for lack of perfection of individual blooms by its profusion of flower.

The pink-flowered magnolias of the *campbellii* group are some of the most magnificent plants that are available for English gardens and in spite of the long time which many of them take to reach flowering size they deserve to be planted more widely than they are. They are hardy enough as plants in practically all parts of England although rather susceptible to exposed positions and cold winds. They are perhaps more suitable for planting in the south and west of England, since there their growth is more rapid and also the chance of their flowers and young growth being all destroyed by frost is less. They have, however, grown and flowered very well in many of the great Sussex gardens, and also in the Great Park at Windsor in both the Savill and the Valley Gardens where they are well worth a visit in late March or early April, depending on the season. There are also some good old specimens at Kew so no one in the south or west of England need be deterred from planting them. A maturing tree of one of these species is a great deterrent to over-frequent house moves.

The earliest to flower and perhaps the finest of these magnolias is *M. campbellii*. Sir Joseph Hooker, writing in the Botanical Magazine last century, described this as 'The noblest specimen of the genus'. It is a forest tree of the Himalaya, growing between eight and ten thousand feet in Sikkim, Bhutan and Nepal, and used to be one of the chief glories of the forests around Darjeeling, forests which I believe are now much sparser than in Hooker's day. There is a most magnificent plate of this magnolia in Hooker and Cathcarts' 'Illustrations of Himalayan Plants'. The bark is dark, almost black, and when in flower all the ends of the branches are covered with flowers, wonderful pink chalices opening gradually into flat plates. The colour is generally deep rose-pink on the outside and inside white, faintly tinged with pink. The flowers are six to ten inches in diameter and have a faint scent. The shape of the unopened flower is graceful as a Chinese pot and as near perfect as any flower can be. In Cornish gardens *Magnolia campbellii* flowers at the end of February and during March, depending on the season, and so in some seasons the flowers are spoilt by spring frosts. However, in those years when February and March bring some beautiful warm sunshine, this magnolia will pay back with over-abundant measure the lengthy years of its youth and the disappointment of other springs. Unfortunately in this country it seldom flowers under twenty years of age and this seems an ineradicable habit.

Imagine, however, a plant with a thousand flowers like pink lotuses or water lilies outlined against a blue sky. The white form is equally beautiful. Some think even more so.

For this reason many may prefer the other pink-flowered species, *M. mollicomata, M. sargentiana* or *M. dawsoniana,* or the fine hybrid between *M. campbellii* and *M. denudata* named *M. veitchii* after the wonderful firm of Veitch where it was raised. *M. veitchii* will often flower after a comparatively few years while *M. mollicomata* and *M. sargentiana,* although taking a long time require perhaps rather less than the age of *M. campbellii* to flower. They have another advantage also in that generally they flower a few weeks later and so have more chance of escaping the spring frosts. In a late season, however, they will all flower together, and sometimes we are able to see all four species at once – an unforgettable experience.

M. mollicomata is very closely allied to *M. campbellii,* in fact it has often been described as the Chinese form of this species. It differs somewhat, however, in its garden behaviour, flowering perhaps as a little younger plant and later; and also in the form of the flowers, which seem rather paler than those of *M. campbellii,* while the outer petals fall away flat and form an outer halo to the central cup. Its flowers are about nine inches across and a good pale pink in colour in the best forms, in others a lilac-pink. It seems to flower more freely than *M. campbellii* and to be a more regular and shapely grower. A fine tree of this, forty feet in height on the edge of a lawn at Trewithen in Cornwall, covered with flower down to the ground, was a sight that I won't quickly forget. The sun was shining on it lighting up the flowers with a translucent pearly glow.

A form called 'Lanarth' after the famous garden where it originated has much darker flowers, a glowing reddish-purple, and is well worth planting if you can get a plant grafted from a scion of the original tree. Seedlings may be more variable in colour. 'Charles Raffill' is raised from a cross between *campbellii* and *mollicomata* at Kew and tends to flower younger than *campbellii.* The flowers are a good deep pink flushed rosy-purple on the outside and very large. Probably the largest flowered

95

seedling of this group is 'Kew's Surprise', but it is still unfortunately a very rare and expensive plant.

Another plant, even out-doing this in floriferousness, is *M. sargentiana* var. *robusta*. It differs from other members of the group in that the huge flowers, sometimes ten inches across, are bent over, with the centre pointing to the horizon or downwards to the earth rather than to the sky, the petals falling apart as the flower opens in a confusion of pink and white with perhaps a touch of mauve and producing an almost unbelievable show of magnificence. The variety *robusta* is more fastigiate and free-flowering and vigorous than the type and is recommended as definitely superior to it.

Magnolia dawsoniana is another wonderful plant of the same group. The flowers seem to have rather a tinge of mauve in them which is not present in the flowers of *M. campbellii*, but it covers itself with flower when fully grown and seems to be lighter in colour than *M. sargentiana*. The petals are rather narrower and more pointed than in the other species and the flower opens rather more loosely. On a visit to Cornwall I saw an old tree flowering on all its top branches and it was a most spectacular sight lit by an evening light and backed by pittosporum and conifers. Unfortunately mature trees of these species are still rare except in the bigger gardens of Cornwall and the west. They should be planted more widely for the future, particularly in parks and public gardens where care may be maintained over a long period.

There is also *M. sprengeri* var. *diva*, which in its best form has pink flowers as deep or deeper than *M. campbellii* and in an old tree they are very freely produced. They are not quite so large as in these other species but they are so numerous that it is a wonderful plant. Its length of time till flowering corresponds more closely to that of *M. mollicomata* or *sargentiana robusta* than to *M. campbellii*, and these have in some gardens flowered under ten years from seed, but this is rare.

The hybrid *M. veitchii* is undoubtedly a very vigorous grower and in the best forms has large pink flowers although not nearly so large as *M. campbellii*, but it flowers very much younger.

(Top) *Cyclamen coum* in January or early February. (H. Smith)

(Centre) Snowdrops at Kew. (H. Smith)

(Bottom left) *Eranthis* x *tubergenii*, a hybrid and the finest winter aconite.

(Bottom right) *Erythronium* 'White Beauty'.

(Top left) *Primula whitei*, a lovely Petiolarid primula. (H. Smith)

(Centre) *Camellia* x *williamsii* 'Donation', one of the most free-flowering camellias. (H. Smith)

(Bottom left) *Skimmia japonica* whose berries last throughout the winter. (H. Smith)

(Bottom right) *Cornus stolinifera* 'Flaviramea' and *C. alba* 'Sibirica'. (H. Smith)

Although the Yulan (*M. denudata*) will seldom flower in the home counties before March is out, it is such a beautiful plant that all who can should have it. In my estimation it is preferable to many of its hybrids of the *soulangeana* group since it always flowers well before the leaves appear, while in some of the hybrids the effect of the flowers tends to be spoilt by the appearance of the young leaves and also by the purple flushing towards the base of the petal. The white goblet flowers create a rare magical effect when a large specimen is floodlit at night. Each flower seems so perfect, so thrilling, even so devastating in its excellence.

Magnolias are really woodland plants and seem to grow best in good yellow loam well mixed with leaf mould and old manure. They resent disturbance and frequently take some years to settle down afterwards. Many authorities prefer to plant in April rather than in the depths of winter so that the roots may go straight ahead. All magnolias seem to appreciate plenty of moisture in the soil as long as it is combined with good drainage, and their vigorous growth requires it. Probably this is a good general recipe for most plants but the water is little use without the drainage and vice versa. It is not general to prune magnolias to any extent except when they are very young or if they get out of shape. Mr Bowles advocated doing any necessary pruning on *M. stellata* in April immediately after flowering. Other authorities advise cutting young plants with rather weak growth down to the base in July so that a really strong shoot or shoots may be produced in the following spring which will be likely to grow away more quickly than the weaker shoots. This can be particularly successful with hybrids such as *M. veitchii* and *soulangeana* provided the young spring shoot can be protected from slugs and other marauding beasts. In the case of the big species such as *M. campbellii*, it may be possible to cut them a little when young so that there are a number of strong shoots and the flowers are not all produced too far up in the sky in the distant day when they do come. Others prefer to keep them to a single trunk as is done at Windsor in the Great Park.

G   97

MAHONIAS

Mahonia japonica, or Berberis as it is still sometimes called, is always in flower for Christmas and continues for two or three months. Like the majority of winter-flowering plants it is not spectacular, but yet it is extremely decorative for the leaves whorl like a windmill, two or three feet in diameter, in the centre of which appear the flowers. These are deep lemon-yellow in colour, and have a most delightful and delicate lemon scent. In size and shape they are like the bells of the lily of the valley, and grow on sprays emerging in succession from the centre of the whirl of leaves and flowering over a long period, opening from the base outwards and spreading almost to the tips of the leaves. This mahonia will make a shrub five feet in height although it is slow growing in the initial stages, and if it is planted in a sunny position the leaves will colour a rich scarlet-crimson in the autumn and will remain on the plant throughout the winter, being tough, only dying when a new whorl comes out in the spring. In shady positions the leaves do not seem to colour much, but remain green through-out the winter. This mahonia is a much more distinctive plant than the common *Mahonia aquifolium*, and is not so rampant since it does not spread with suckers underground. It is easily propagated from cuttings.

We owe the first discovery of this fine plant to Robert Fortune who found it in a deserted garden in southern Anhwei, when he was on his expedition to collect tea seeds so that China tea might be grown in India, a fruitless attempt. The shrub was about eight feet high and much branched, and as Fortune remarked: 'It had but one fault and that was that it was too large to move and bring away'. All berberis and mahonias resent very much any move when they are big. The Chinese believed that it had some potent medical power, and he had great difficulty in persuading them to part with plants. How-ever, he managed to bring three young plants, and from these our stock has been propagated.

The species with the spreading flowers which I have described has often been distributed under the name of *M. japonica* var. *bealei* or just *Mahonia bealei*, but this name really belongs to a separate species with shorter upright flower spikes and the one with the spreading racemes is *Mahonia japonica* and is certainly the better garden plant of the two.

Another species which was more recently introduced is *M. lomariifolia*. It has upright spikes of deeper yellow flowers growing in large clusters in early winter, often opening first in November but lasting in flower sometimes for two months. The flowers are probably not quite so frost resistant as those of *M. japonica* but it would be worth growing for its finely divided foliage alone. Each leaflet of the long leaf is like that of a holly but with a fresher more yellow green. It is certainly a plant of distinction. Although it was found as low as four thousand feet in north Burma it has proved hardy in a number of English gardens, and I have seen plants ten feet in height and rivalling plants photographed by Kingdon Ward in their native habitat. It should if possible, though, be grown in a warm and protected position when away from the south and west of the country. I well remember one superb specimen in the Midlands in a sheltered corner, protected by two walls of a big house. It was eight or ten feet high with several stems, and in front was *Cotoneaster conspicuus* covered in red berries, an excellent combination.

A hybrid between *M. japonica* and *M. lomariifolia* has been named 'Charity' and probably in garden value surpasses both its parents. It is a tall growing plant with leaves up to two feet in length, well divided like those of its parents between which it is intermediate. It usually starts flowering about mid-November and continues for two months, being very resistant to frost. The flowers seem more numerous than those of *M. japonica* and stand more upright so that they make a large head. Its only disadvantage is that if left unpruned it tends to get rather tall and leggy, but it will generally sprout if cut back half way. Young plants should be encouraged to branch low down by nipping out the growing bud at about two feet. Plants of this group vary slightly and several clones have been

99

separated, notably 'Hope' after Mr Hope Findlay of the Savill Garden and 'Buckland' after the home of Mr Lionel Fortescue who raised it independently.

The species with the largest and finest leaves of all is *M. acanthifolia* but it is more tender than the others mentioned. The leaves can reach three feet in length and are borne in a whorl near the top of the stems. *M. napaulensis* is also a handsome plant close to *M. japonica* in its characters and it makes quite a large shrub, those I have seen in gardens being much finer than those I have seen in the wild in Nepal.

A large patch of the common *M. aquifolium* with its bright yellow flowers is also a good investment for the wild garden, making splendid ground cover. I have often used it also for picking in early March and on into April, while its holly-like foliage will colour brilliantly in the autumn and last so for much of the winter if planted in a sunny position. *M. pinnata* is also an excellent foliage plant close to *M. aquifolium* but usually a little taller and stiffer in growth. 'Undulata', with wavy-edged leaves, is probably a hybrid between these two.

RHODODENDRONS

The winter-flowering rhododendrons seem to be relatively little known, yet several of them are most desirable plants. The range is considerable in the case of the more sheltered gardens along the south coast and in the west, but nevertheless there are several which will grow well in the home counties and flower freely. Their actual flowers and the buds, once the colour is showing, are susceptible to frost, but in many years a mild spell will last long enough to get them through the bud stage into flower and if the young growth is cut later it is likely that they will make more.

Probably the earliest to flower is *Rhododendron mucronulatum*, a purple-flowered species which serves as the perfect foil for the yellow *Hamamelis mollis*, the two flowering together in January. It is a deciduous species, producing the flowers in clusters towards the end of the branches. They are rather more open and salver-shaped than in many of the larger flowering hybrids, and one and a half to two inches in diameter. While not a dwarf for the rock garden alone, *R. mucronulatum* seldom forms a very large shrub. About four to five feet is the normal height. In bud it is very resistant to frost and if one crop of flowers should be destroyed it will frequently produce a second.

Another purple-flowering rhododendron which will follow *R. mucronulatum* in February or March is *R. praecox*, a hybrid between *R. dauricum* and *R. ciliatum*. The flowers are a light rosy-mauve, but in some forms and some lights appear almost pink. It is a very easily grown plant and in the bud stage completely resistant to frost, and opens into flower only a very few days after the tight buds burst. At Edinburgh Botanic Garden a hedge of this rhododendron has been planted and is a magnificent sight when in bloom. The flowers are not very large, about an inch to an inch and a half in diameter, but they are borne in clusters. This forms a neat, rather tight-growing rhododendron, generally not over three to four feet in height. It is very free flowering, often lasting in flower for several weeks, and a plant worthy of a place in every garden where the soil is lime free.

In our category also come two attractive white and creamy-white species, which are both good plants in themselves and have served as good parents. Probably the best of these is *R. moupinense* and often this flowers magnificently during February. It is of rather a dwarf habit and flowers when the plant is quite small, and is well worth a sheltered place in the large rock garden or on the edge of the woodland garden. The protection it requires is that from the early morning sun as well as that from north and east winds. The flowers are large, often over two inches across, white in colour, with crimson markings towards the base, and are borne in small, rather loose, clusters. There is also a pink-flowering form. While not quite so frost resistant as the two previously mentioned plants, it is still very well worth growing in most counties. My other species is *R. leucaspis*, and it is not quite so frost resistant in bud as *R. moupinense,* but still a desirable plant for any sheltered position. *R. leucaspis* is a dwarf rhododendron with comparatively large cream flowers which open wide to show chocolate-coloured anthers. It flowers in a few years from seed and is also an excellent plant for the alpine house, where it should flower safely each year. Another attractive feature of this plant is the pink scales of the buds and the neat hairy leaves. It flowers in February and March. It was collected by Kingdon Ward in the Tsangpo gorge of Tibet.

One of the finest of the hybrids which these two species have yielded is R. 'Cilpinense', a cross between *R. moupinense* and *R. ciliatum.* The plant is a neat dwarf grower with most attractive shining glossy leaves and buds, tightly wrapped in pink scales. The flowers are very pale pink and are magnificent during mild spells in March. This is a plant which should be grown much more frequently, as should also its parent *R. ciliatum* which has both pink and white forms. Another newer hybrid which is a very useful addition to our winter-flowering plants is R. 'Bric-à-Brac', a cross between *R. moupinense* and *R. leucaspis* which seems to combine the more desirable characteristics of both parents. The plant is a dwarf grower and stiffer in growth than *R. moupinense,* and the flowers are large and creamy-white as those of *R. leucaspis,* while retaining the size of the flowers of *R. moupinense.* It flowers early in March, slightly before R. 'Cilpinense'.

A March-flowering species, which we have not yet mentioned, is *R. lutescens,* a rather loose-growing shrub with pale yellow flowers. It is one of the commonest and best known of the very early flowering rhododendrons and is well worth planting freely in groups wherever there is space. A single plant is inclined not to make enough effect. The finest form is probably that selected by Exbury, to which the First Class Certificate was awarded, but it is tender outside the milder areas. Rather hardier but not quite such a deep yellow is 'Bagshot Sands'. The young foliage has delightful bronze tints in it. The hybrid between this species and *R. moupinense* has been christened 'Bo-Peep' and is a delightful plant, rather more reminiscent of *lutescens* than *moupinense*.

Two of the plants that I would hate to lose from the winter garden are 'Tessa Roza' and 'Seta', two magnificent hybrids flowering in late February or March and growing to a height of three to four feet usually. 'Tessa Roza' is the best form of the 'Tessa' cross between *R. moupinense* and *R.* x *praecox* and is, I think, preferable to either of its parents. The flowers are pale pinkish-purple and open almost flat up to about two and a half inches across. The young growth is also bronzy and attractive. 'Seta' makes a more compact bush, covered with buds every year and flowering successfully in most years. The flowers are pale shell-pink, deeper at the tips, rather long and tubular since it is a cross between *R. moupinense* and *R. spinuliferum*. 'Chink', a cross between *R. keiskei* and *R. trichocladum*, is also worth growing, a dwarfer, compact plant with greenish-yellow flowers in March.

All the species and hybrids we have so far mentioned are small-leaved rather dwarf plants, but there is also a number of larger leaved winter and very early spring flowering species and hybrids which are especially valuable in the west of England, but a few of which may be successful in the home counties. Probably the best known of these is R. 'Nobleanum' which in a suitable situation and season may be in flower by Christmas. In form it resembles one of the late flowering hybrids with rather a tight truss of flower and leaves which are covered beneath with rust-coloured indumentum. It is a hybrid between *R. arboreum* and *R. caucasicum* and there are white forms, pink forms and deep crimson forms. Although this is one of our oldest hybrids it is still little known. Two other old hybrids, 'Christmas Cheer' and 'Jacksoni', are also derived from *R. caucasicum*, very tough and flowering in early March and therefore still worth growing where there is space, although the pink flowers will not compare in size or quality with later flowering hybrids. *R. arboreum* has formed handsome trees forty feet or more in height in many gardens in the west of Scotland and the west of England and is a most striking spectacle when covered with pink or crimson flowers in February. Its best blood-red forms, however, are definitely rather tender away from the west and it is also sensitive to summer droughts, but in some Cornish gardens it has grown forty or more feet high and is really magnificent in flower.

A slightly tougher species is *R. barbatum* with hairy bases to the leaves and bright scarlet, pink or crimson flowers in very tight buds in March. Both this and the previous species have been long in cultivation in this country, many having been grown from Hooker's seed collected in the Himalayas in the first half of the last century and having by now developed into large trees and yielded a number of distinct colour forms. The true species of *R. barbatum* has blood-red flowers borne in a compact truss four inches or so across. This, of course, will not compare in size with the larger flowering May and June hybrids but still a March-flowering plant must not be judged by the same standards as a June-flowering one, and I find the very bright reds more acceptable at this season. It also has the finest bark in the genus, a beautiful cinnamon-purple and quite smooth when last year's has peeled off. A rather larger flowered hybrid between *R. barbatum* and *R. thomsonii* is *Rhododendron* 'Shilsoni' and I think this deserves to be more frequently grown than it is, especially in the west of England, as does also the lovely 'Red Admiral', produced at Caerhays from *R. thomsonii*. The flowers of both are deep blood-red. The two clones of R. 'Barclayi' known as 'Helen Fox' and 'Robert Fox,' flowering in March with large trusses of deep scarlet or crimson flowers, are very fine in Cornwall and the milder counties and make large bushes or even trees but are too tender elsewhere.

Another large-leaved species is *R. sutchuenense* which has large heads of pinkish-mauve flowers in early March. The upper lobes of the flowers are spotted crimson and the whole effect is attractive, the flower clusters often being eight inches across. This species will also grow into a large tree in favoured situations, but has the great advantage of flowering when quite small. Probably the finest form is that called *geraldii* which has deep rose-pink flowers with a chocolate blotch at the base of the corolla. Both this species and *R. barbatum* have been classified H3-4 for hardiness in the Rhododendron Handbook which should encourage all except those with the coldest gardens to grow them.

In a mild winter *R. oreodoxa* makes a very lovely tree dripping with delicate pink bell-like flowers in March and it is one of my favourites although it will not always flower in the season of this book. *R. eclecteum* and *R. stewartianum* will also usually flower in March, and the colour of their flower is very variable between a good creamy-yellow and a deep pink. These are especially plants for the woodland garden, that form of gardening which perhaps yields the greatest return for the least labour. Also the naturalness of the well designed woodland garden seems to bring more peace and relaxation to me than the old formal garden of bedding plants.

VIBURNUMS

There are few plants so waxy and so sweet smelling as the winter-flowering viburnums. A small vase in a room is stronger and sweeter than a visit to a Paris scent shop. The earliest species to flower is *Viburnum farreri*, but still better known as *V. fragrans*, which will often be in bloom by November if the season is mild. It is wonderfully resistant to frost as well. This plant makes a thick shrub, in the oldest specimens as much as eight foot in height and as much through, and will continue flowering throughout the winter. The young buds are pale pink but the flowers open almost pure white and are borne in clusters often two inches or more across. The only disadvantage of this viburnum, and it applies to the majority of the members of the genus, is its essential shapelessness. I have never seen a *Viburnum farreri* grown into a plant of any form and if one tried to trim it into a more shapely plant one would probably have to cut off much of the flower bud. Perhaps the best solution is to grow it in a group of several plants which will grow together and produce a kind of umbrella-shaped thicket. Mr E. A. Bowles used to grow just such a group underplanted with *Cyclamen neapolitanum* and with a background of dark conifers and it was most successful. Although known to botanists for some time previously, *V. farreri* was only introduced to cultivation by Farrer from Kansu. It had long been known as a cultivated plant in Chinese gardens, but Farrer found it there growing wild in the scrub of the hillsides and he wrote in his notes: 'Here this most glorious of flowering shrub is genuinely indigenous'. However, he collected his seed from temple gardens and would have sent more except for an unfortunate misunderstanding with the Prince of Joni, who 'to avenge himself, set to and sedulously ate up all the viburnum fruit in his palace garden and threw away the seed'. There are two forms of *V. farreri* in English gardens, one with slightly bronzed foliage and pink buds, the other with green foliage and white buds. The former, I feel, is the more desirable. There is also the dwarf form, but it is not usually very free flowering.

Viburnum grandiflorum, which has forms with quite deep pink flowers and others with white flowers with a pinkish flush on the bare boughs in January and February, can be superior to *V. farreri* in milder gardens and I have seen some splendid bushes; but in other gardens, although hardy enough as a shrub, it does not seem to flower freely or as a young plant. The flower heads are slightly larger than those of *V. farreri* and in the pink forms show a good deal more colour. The flowers are slightly drooping. I remember seeing it high up in a valley in Nepal flowering near patches of melting snow in June, but the wild forms there were not the equal of some of the best ones I have seen in cultivation.

Probably even better than either of these species for the home counties and gardens outside the south or west coast areas is *V.* x *bodnantense*, a hybrid between the two which has slightly more substantial flower heads than *V. farreri*. It flowers over the same season. When out, the flowers last much better in water than those of *V. farreri* which tend to drop quickly, and they have the same glorious scent. The seedlings are, however, variable and the best ones to get are 'Dawn', the finest of the original clones raised at Bodnant which has pink-flushed flowers, and 'Deben' which has much whiter flower heads. Both are very resistant to some frost in flower although of course will be browned by a strong air frost like nearly all flowers.

Another good species of the same group is *V. foetens* although it is rarely seen. It has clusters of white flowers again appearing before the leaves but usually not till early March. It has one great advantage also in that the flower heads appear all together while in the other species mentioned some of the effect tends to be frittered away, especially in a mild winter, by the flowers appearing intermittently whenever a mild spell stimulates them.

Viburnum carlesii is another plant which should be in every garden. Flowering later than *V. farreri* and generally not until March, it is yet even waxier and sweeter and the flowers are borne in larger clusters. In bud the flowers are a delightful cherry-red which is not seen when they open, since inside the petals are pure white. The buds are formed in autumn, so that a warm period in early spring will bring it into flower, although after a severe winter it may not flower till April. It is a more compact grower. Discovered in Korea by a consul named Charles in 1883, it was only introduced to this country in 1902 and then from a plant collected in Japan, probably from a garden. There have also been several good hybrid viburnums raised and the best of these is *V. burkwoodii*, a plant also of strong perfume which I can heartily recommend. It forms a large loose-growing shrub and flowers more freely with us than either *V. farreri* or *V. carlesii*. The flowers are rather similar to those of *V. carlesii* but are often borne spasmodically through the winter months with the final main crop in March or early April. The buds, however, lack the colour of *V. carlesii*. We have picked our first in November. It is also a semi-evergreen, being a hybrid between *V. carlesii* and *V. utile*. The best forms of this cross are 'Anne Russell' and 'Park Farm Hybrid' although they may flower slightly later than the type.

The common Laurustinus (*Viburnum tinus*) is a useful and regular winter-flowering shrub, but the type has always failed to thrill me, being mentally classed with laurels and aucubas, and I do not grow it in my own garden. There are, however, some finer forms although they are a little more tender. These are *lucidum* with looser more vigorous growth and larger heads of rather whiter flowers, 'Eve Price', a selected form with pinker flowers and dense compact habit and 'French White' with almost pure white flowers. It is splendid in Riviera gardens but rarely seen in English ones, although it is worth trying in the milder areas. *V. rhytidophyllum* is also a very useful plant for winter effect. Its large leaves are evergreen, heavily veined and covered underneath with a thick rust-coloured indumentum, not unlike those of *Rhododendron falconeri*.

All viburnums like a strong soil enriched and mulched at intervals and they seem to prefer an open sunny situation. They require no regular pruning although they will flower better if the very old and worn out stems are cut out from time to time. This is probably best done after flowering time in April and will encourage the growth of stronger shoots from the base.

WILLOWS

The early willows have the great quality of softness in their flower heads, a silvery soft fluffy nature which makes them sparkle in the sunlight and invites one to stroke them as one strokes the soft fur of a cat.

The earliest willow to produce its catkins is *Salix aegyptiaca*, formerly and probably still more frequently known as *S. medemii*. It does not at any rate come from Egypt but rather from the mountains of southern Russia and is absolutely hardy. It often begins to flower in January and continues over a long season. It is also excellent for cutting for the house to mix with stylosa irises. The catkins are quite large and silvery.

Probably the best species for later flowering is *S. daphnoides*, the young twigs of which are coloured a rich plum-purple overlaced with a delicate white bloom. For this alone they would be attractive in winter but in early spring, often in February, the silver catkins will burst forth from the buds, increasing in size and silveriness till Easter. They are magnificent decoration for the house and cutting will keep this rather loose-growing form in good shape. In size and form it resembles the native *S. caprea*, the 'palm' of our Easter ceremonies. A fine selected form of this is 'Aglaia' which has very large male catkins early in the year but the twigs do not have quite so much bloom. Like so many of our finest winter-flowering plants the willows look best against a dark background. *S. daphnoides* and *S. caprea* do not need to be grown by water. I also like *S. gracilistyla* which has grey downy young shoots and smaller catkins but they are equally early in flower and the whole is slenderer and more delicate in form. Like the others, it can be pruned hard in the spring to make plenty of young shoots since these usually give the best catkins. Close to this is *S. melanostachys* in which the catkins at first appear almost black and then open to show the red anthers.

The weeping willows also do not need to be planted by water, but are generally seen to best advantage beside water and certainly thrive best in a damp position. In spring they are almost the earliest of deciduous trees to show any signs of leaf, and at the end of February or during March begin to show a shimmer of palest yellow-green which quickly develops into a buoyant fountain of pale colour which assures us that spring is really coming. I know of no plant more suggestive of the idea of spring and all that we associate with that period of rebirth. The finest form to plant is *Salix alba vitellina pendula*, sometimes known as *S. chrysocoma*, and this has received the award of garden merit. It is often sold under the name of *S. babylonica ramulis aureis*. It is very free growing and the twigs are bright yellow, sweeping down almost to the ground in an old specimen. Even throughout the winter it adds colour to the garden.

Colour in bark and stem is a most valuable winter character and one which is much neglected by gardeners. There is the

109

wonderful whiteness of certain birches, the rich almost polished
mahogany of certain cherries and maples, the brilliant sealing-
wax scarlet of the young stems of the best forms of cornus and
the fine young red and orange twigs of forms of willow. These
willows are best planted in a damp situation, and may be cut
down almost to a foot of the ground each spring so that they
grow up in a thick mass of young twigs. Lit up by the winter
sun against a dark background of yews, a group of these red-
twigged willows will present a very brilliant effect, one that
will last right through the winter. Probably the best is the
cardinal willow, *S. alba* 'Chermesina' still sometimes known as
S. vitellina britzensis. S. irrorata has a pleasant silvery-white
bloom on the twigs which is very conspicuous in winter and
makes a good contrast.

All varieties of willow root easily from slips inserted in a
damp place or even in a bottle of water during the late summer.
It is related that many of the weeping willows in this country
have been grown from slips taken from those round the tomb
of Napoleon on St Helena when all ships touched there on
their way back from the Cape and the Far East. These slips
just had time to root nicely during the voyage home in a
bottle of water.

The weeping willow and *Salix babylonica* are naturally
associated with the grief of the Israelites and their harps.
Linnaeus believed this to be the tree but he did not visit the
Euphrates. Later authorities, however, have asserted that the
trees of the psalm are really poplars, *Populus euphratica*, while
the native habitat of the weeping willow is China. It probably
came to us, however, via Turkey. In the spring it is bright and
anything but melancholy.

A little known but very beautiful willow is *Salix fargesii*,
which has shorter branches than the previous species, with the
young wood shining a deep crimson as if covered with sealing-
wax or varnish, out of which appear the silvery buds like
spear-heads, a delightful combination. It is hardy enough in
most situations and is a good shrub for the south and west.

Some Other Good Winter Plants

ABELIOPHYLLUM DISTICHUM

This comparatively recent introduction from Korea deserves to be better known, for in a favourable season it will begin to flower in January. A twiggy loose-growing shrub, it can be grown either in the open or against a south wall; probably the latter is preferable except in the mild counties of the south-west. The flowers are white, tubular and nearly as large as those of a forsythia and somewhat similar in form. They are borne in clusters on short side shoots towards the end of the main branches. They are very spicily fragrant and last well if cut and brought into the house. It is important to prune these hard after flowering, cutting out all the flowering shoots nearly to their base so that plenty of young twiggy shoots are produced for next year's flowering. I have seen specimens absolutely covered with flower. The generic name is derived from the form of the leaves and not from any other close affinity with *Abelias*.

ACACIAS

There is nothing more delightful and spring-like in the midst of winter than the great bunches of fluffy yellow Mimosa which one sees in the streets. Alas, how short a time they remain fluffy in our warm houses. The correct name for the common mimosa is *Acacia dealbata*. In the milder counties of the south and west by the sea it can be grown out of doors with a reasonable chance of success, and big plants have been grown in Surrey in very specially sheltered positions, as may be witnessed by the large one at Wisley which grew in the corner formed by the porch and the laboratory wall. In recent seasons, however, this has suffered very severely and has been cut to the ground.

It needs a sheltered position where it can be baked a bit in summer, as happens on the Riviera. At Dartington Hall in Devonshire it is wonderful covering a whole wall. In cool greenhouses or conservatories it can be grown without difficulty, but must be cut back regularly in order to keep it within bounds and avoid a very lanky plant with all the growth against the top glass. It needs also regular care to keep it clean from mealy bugs and other pests.

Another species of great charm is *Acacia baileyana*, which has flowers of the same golden yellow but glaucous almost blue foliage. It is slightly more tender than the common mimosa. Another species which is very nearly hardy is *Acacia armata*, the Kangaroo Thorn. This does not grow nearly so large and is very suitable for the small greenhouse since it makes a twiggy, prickly, rather rounded bush with masses of yellow flowers in the spring and fresh yellowish-green foliage.

ADONIS

Although delighting in one of the most magnificent names in plant life, *Adonis* are rarely seen in English gardens. They are desirable and useful plants although by no means as distinguished as their name implies. Adonis is often called 'Flower of the Gods' and the legend traces the origin to the drops of blood of Adonis after he had been wounded by a wild beast. This presumably refers to the annual *Adonis aestivalis* which has deep scarlet-red flowers which glow blood-like in the late summer. The winter-flowering kinds are perennial and have yellow buttercup-like flowers two inches or more across borne in the centre of a tuft of finely divided foliage. The best kind is *Adonis vernalis* which flowers in March and is only six inches or so in height.

The other species sometimes grown is *A. amurensis* from Manchuria which has taller flowers early in March. There are, however, several varieties ranging in colour from cream through deep yellow through orange to a buff-pink, and some a coppery-red. They are great favourites with Japanese gardeners who

Mahonia 'Charity', often begins to flower in late November. (J. E. Downward)

Rhododendron 'Seta', has pale pink flowers in February or March and hardly ever fails to flower except when the buds are frosted as they open. (J. E. Downward)

have bred and selected many forms, and use them for decorating their houses on New Year's Day, but few are seen in English gardens. There is an excellent article about them in the R.H.S. Journal for March 1964. The Japanese recommend that they should be kept cool in summer, avoiding dryness when they are dormant. There is also a double *Adonis*, *A. wolgensis*, with yellow flowers tipped with green and very finely divided fern-like foliage. It is persistent and flowers well each year in February or early March on the north-facing slope near the top of the rock garden at Wisley.

Adonis like a sunny position and require no very special cultivation. They need, however, to be left undisturbed for several years after planting before they form really fine flowering clumps.

ALNUS

The alders are seldom planted for effect, but when cut the catkins make a most attractive decoration for the house, while there are also two closely related varieties, *Alnus incana* 'Aurea' with yellowish-red young shoots and yellow foliage in spring, and *A. incana* 'Ramulis Coccineis' with reddish-scarlet young twigs which can make a very striking effect and serve to light up parts of the winter garden. These are usually sold as grafted plants and I have found them difficult to establish, the grafts not often being very firm in young plants. The Grey alder, *A. incana* itself, and the Italian alder *A. cordata* both make handsome trees and are rather more distinctive in foliage than our common alder. Their yellowish-green catkins are also a little longer. The yellow drooping catkins are the male flowers: the female are borne in short upright conical branches and are not very conspicuous. Some prefer to grow the cut leaved forms of our native and of the grey alder *A. glutinosa* 'Imperialis' or 'Laciniata', and *A. incana* 'Laciniata', but this will not make any difference to their winter effect.

* * *

ARBUTUS

The arbutus is particularly distinguished for its decorative form of growth and wonderful bark colour throughout the year and is discussed under the chapter on bark in the winter garden, but it also flowers and fruits in winter. For these characters the European strawberry tree, *Arbutus unedo*, is very fine. The flowers are urn-shaped and hang in large clusters among the dark leathery foliage, in the type greenish-white flushed pink; in the variety 'Rubra' a deeper pink. They usually open first in October and remain on the tree for most of the winter. At the same time the fruit ripens and hangs like little red round strawberries for much of the winter. The flowers of *A. andrachnoides*, the hybrid with *A. andrachne*, are very similar and this tree has better bark, thus making it perhaps the first choice in the genus. The fruits of the American Madrono, *A. menziesii*, also hang in large clusters from more upright panicles and vary from orange to a deep crimson, each being the size of a pea. It is a splendid tree also for its bark. The flowers, however, open in spring rather than in winter.

BERGENIAS

These are decorative plants both for their flower and their foliage. From January onwards there are usually some flowers out on the common bergenia although the main flowering is usually not before March and early April, and this later flowering applies to some of the choicer varieties such as 'Ballawley', a form of *B. purpurascens* with the most superb and massive foliage in the genus. The leaves tend to turn purplish-red in autumn and so last for much of the winter. The flowers are bright purplish-red and stand up on foot-length stems in large clusters. The bergenias used to be regarded as part of the genus *Saxifraga* under the section *Megasea* but they seem to me well separated as a genus on their own. They make excellent ground cover and their large shining leathery leaves alone make them worth a space and they will do well in semi-shade although they flower better in the open.

CHAENOMELES

This old favourite has in recent years masqueraded under an ever-lengthening series of names, but is often called just 'Japonica'; in the more recent books it is now described as *Chaenomeles*. The name *Cydonia* under which the species were long known is now usually kept just for the quinces under the name *C. oblonga* and they flower too late for discussion here. The 'Japonicas' will mostly now be found under *Chaenomeles speciosa* or *C. superba* which is a hybrid group derived from *C. japonica* x *C. speciosa*. If planted in the open they will form large bushes with many young shoots always growing from the base and flowering freely on the older wood. Against a wall they flower even more freely and can be pruned of much of their superfluous wood so that the older branches are trained back against the wall when they will cover themselves with flowers from February to April, depending on the season. An attractive pink variety of *C. speciosa* is 'Phylis Moore' named after a very charming and distinguished Irish gardener, while 'Moerloosii' is rather similar but paler with pink and white flowers. The commoner forms are mostly the scarlets and the orange-scarlet and belong under *C. superba*. Of the pure scarlet I can recommend 'Knaphill Scarlet' or 'Rowallane' in both of which the flowers are large, those of 'Rowallane' being the deeper red. Of the orange-reds *C. japonica* itself is still the one most commonly grown. Others I like are 'Cardinalis', deep scarlet-crimson' and 'Nivalis', pure white, both forms of *C. speciosa*. Less conspicuous in flower but distinguished for its vast fruits often four inches or more long is *C. cathayensis*. The fruits, yellowish-green in colour, last on the bush through much of the winter and are quite decorative as well as making excellent jelly. All the chaenomeles are very resistant to frosts, particularly as wall plants, and it needs to be a very hard air frost to damage them. As shrubs in the open they tend to be rather formless and need most of the young suckers taking out from the base and quite hard pruning, otherwise they just become a shapeless tangle for which the flowers hardly compensate.

CHIMONANTHUS PRAECOX

This is one of the standard winter-flowering plants. It cannot be described as spectacular in any way, but it has one of the sweetest scents which is particularly strong when a branch is cut and brought into a warm room: in fact it is frequently known as the 'Winter Sweet'. *Chimonanthus* is a rather slow growing shrub, but in time it will reach eight or more feet in height. It is not necessary to plant it against a wall, but if this is done, probably the wood is better ripened in the summer and the flowers open slightly earlier. It generally blooms from December to February and is one of the most reliable of all winter flowers. The blossoms are straw-coloured and hang rather clawlike from short shoots along the growth of the current year. They are about an inch in diameter and the inner segments carry purplish markings, which are not, however, very conspicuous, being hidden by the drooping claws of the outer segments. The variety 'Grandiflorus' has slightly larger flowers with a trace more yellow in the straw, but it is not quite so fragrant. The most conspicuous form in flower is undoubtedly 'Luteus' and it has been known since the early years of the nineteenth century. The flowers are a good lemon-yellow but again the scent is not so strong as in the type. However, it is certainly the one I would choose to grow in a small garden. Little pruning is generally necessary on bushes, but on wall plants the older wood should be cut out after flowering to encourage new growth. *Chimonanthus* is difficult to propagate from cuttings, but may be layered.

CLEMATIS

There are two clematis which flower within our season: *C.*

cirrhosa, from the Mediterranean region, flowers from January to March with creamy or greenish-white drooping bell-like flowers two or three inches across, generally in pairs; the other is *C. cirrhosa* var. *balearica* whose range extends from Majorca to Corsica, and it flowers spasmodically throughout the winter. The flowers are rather similar in size and colouring although with some red spotting towards the centre, but it has an added advantage in that its foliage is very finely divided and turns bronzy in winter. It is, however, slightly the more tender of the two and both should be grown in a warm sunny position.

CORNUS

The Cornelian cherry, is nearly always covered with a fluffy mass of small yellow flowers in February or early March and is a most desirable plant. It forms a large shrub up to ten feet in height with a rounded twiggy head. The clusters of little flowers are produced when the bush is leafless and are bright sulphur-yellow in colour with small petals and prominent masses of stamens. The bright red berries are not regularly borne in this country but on the continent and in North America are used for jam. They are about the size of rose hips. This cornus is one of the easiest and most satisfactory of winter-flowering plants and is worth a place in every garden. It appreciates a sunny position. Unfortunately *Cornus chinensis*, a very exciting plant collected by Kingdon Ward in Upper Burma and much heralded as a larger-flowered *C. mas*, has proved too tender outside for most gardens in this country and too large for all greenhouses except the largest. The scarlet barked forms of dogwood are mentioned in the chapter on bark. They are very valuable in winter. They are not forms of *Cornus sanguinea* whose name refers to the autumn foliage solely, but forms of *Cornus alba*.

CORYLOPSIS

The pale yellow pendulous spikes of corylopsis flowers are a delightful decoration from late February till early April. In form and leaf character the corylopsis resemble the hazels, although they belong to the *Hamamelis* family as do the Witch Hazels. They are perfectly hardy and the flowers are borne before the leaves. The individual flowers are small, but they are pleasantly scented, some say like cowslips, and the clusters are often several inches in length while each flower has a pale straw-coloured bract at its base. The anthers are crimson which gives just that extra touch of warmer colour to the flowers and prevents them from seeming too insipid. The most commonly grown species is *Corylopsis spicata* and this is perfectly hardy although the flowers may occasionally be damaged by late frosts. They are natives of China and Japan and other good species are *C. pauciflora*, a much dwarfer shrub with pale yellow flowers and shorter spikes, and *C. veitchiana* which is a good shrub of more recent introduction but it appears to be slightly more tender than *C. spicata*. The yellow autumn colour of *C. spicata* is also decorative in some seasons, though it cannot be described as one of our strongest colourers. On visits to the south-west I have been much attracted by *C. sinensis* and *C. platypetala*, whose flower clusters seemed rather longer than those of the previously mentioned species, and they seem to grow quite well in the Valley Gardens in Windsor Great Park. There are some enormous specimens of *C. platypetala* in Cornish gardens.

FATSIA JAPONICA AND FATSHEDERA

Fatsia is one of the most decorative members of the ivy family and flowers in this country from October to November. It can be grown well in the southern counties and in the south-west of England, and I have seen some good plants five foot high and as much across in London gardens. It does best, however, in a sheltered place. The flowers are pale green, sometimes almost white, and are borne in large rounded heads at the ends of the branches. The leaves are very large, palmate and deeply lobed, somewhat like those of *Ricinus* the Castor Oil plant, and being a light but shining green are very decorative in the right setting, and when cut act as a good foil for flowers of brighter colouring. Sometimes they are a foot or more in length and nearly as much across.

Fatshedera lizei is a bigeneric hybrid between an ivy and *Fatsia*, and is an equally decorative plant, flowering in late October and throughout November with big upright panicles of greenish-white ivy-like flowers. It does not usually grow so tall as the *Fatsia* but tends to sprawl over the ground more loosely. As a house plant the 'Fat-headed Lizzie', as it is often known, is very popular but it is hardy enough in sheltered positions outside.

FORSYTHIAS

The earliest to flower of the forsythias is *F. giraldiana*, not so spectacular a plant as the later species and hybrids, but still very well worth growing for its early season. Generally the beginning of a warm March will see it in flower. It is often rather a straggly bush and the flowers are rather paler in colour than in the better known forsythias, but it seems to be rather a variable plant. The next to flower is *F. ovata* with rather small yellow flowers, usually solitary, but with a charm of its own. It is quickly followed by *F. x. intermedia* and *F. suspensa* and the commonest variety F. 'Spectabilis'. This is the forsythia usually grown and is certainly the freest flowering of all and the strongest in colour, the branches being literally covered by the golden bells. I like also 'Beatrix Farrand' and 'Lynwood', both of which have slightly larger deep yellow flowers, and *F. suspensa atrocaulis* which has black stems and paler lemon flowers. Except in a favourable early season their main display, though, will be in early April rather than in March. A big bush or a thicket of several bushes lights up any garden at a season when we are still very glad of flowers. All the forsythias strike very readily from cuttings and grow rapidly in almost any position, though in a sunny one they form bushes of a better shape. They should all be pruned immediately they have finished flowering, the older flowering wood being removed.

GARRYA ELLIPTICA

The long catkins of Garrya, clothed in a suede-like grey, elegant and soft, hang often for months from midwinter till late spring. The finest catkins are the male ones and the two sexes are borne on different plants. The shrubs are evergreen, the leaves being rather leathery and dark in colour and possibly this conduces to the slightly melancholy appearance of garrya. I often wonder how the branches would look cut and stripped of their leaves: I believe they would be most decorative. In spite of this, garrya is a valuable winter-flowering plant which seldom fails. It is a Californian plant, but even so is reasonably hardy and in a good position, perhaps slightly sheltered, will form a large bush. It is definitely a plant that requires careful placing, the effect of the catkins being lost against too dark a background. They are very freely borne and often are six inches or more in length. For a short period the stamens will be visible as little yellow frilly bands at intervals down the catkins, and it is sometimes known most appropriately as the Tassel Bush.

HEBE

These are the shrubby veronicas of most old lists and they have a very long season of flower, often prolonged from late autumn till January or even February depending on the season and the situation. They are also good foliage plants. They seem to grow particularly well by the seaside, being tolerant of wind. 'Midsummer Beauty' with its long spikes of pale mauve flowers and 'Autumn Glory' with its more dense habit and stronger violet-blue flowers will generally carry on well into the winter months, but the most prolific then are forms of *H. speciosa*, particularly the deep pink ones such as 'Gauntletti', 'Evelyn' and 'La Seduisante' which is rather more purple. The richest crimson is 'Simon Delaux' but it seems to be more tender and is not so often seen. All can easily be preserved over winter by taking a pot of cuttings in the autumn and keeping them in a cool greenhouse or even on a window ledge. These are not, however, suitable plants for the very cold garden or the one in a frost pocket and in others may need renewing occasionally after a very severe winter. They grow easily from cuttings.

HONEYSUCKLES

The winter-flowering honeysuckles seem to be all bushes rather than climbers. *Lonicera fragrantissima* is one of the best of these and the small white or cream coloured flowers, usually in pairs, are very fragrant and, being frost resistant, seem to send out their scent as they thaw out into the surrounding air. A few sprays will also scent a room. It flowers very early in the year, often beginning in December and continuing till March. The leaves usually persist through the winter and consequently somewhat hide the flowers, which are borne in their axils. They are nearly an inch in length and generally grow in pairs. This plant does not make any of the fine display of the later flowering twining honeysuckles, but its scent is undeniable and for that reason it is worth growing in a sunny position. If wall space is available, so much the better.

Slightly larger in flower but not so fragrant is *Lonicera standishii*. The flowers vary from white to cream and are rather more conspicuous since the leaves are less persistent. However, I would prefer the former species of the two since the scent is the character for which these honeysuckles are grown. Both of these species were found by Robert Fortune in eastern China and distributed through the R.H.S. There is also a hybrid between these two, *L.* x *purpusii*, with very similar characteristics but perhaps a little more vigour and more freedom of flowering than its parents, and some regard it as the best of the winter-flowering honeysuckles.

OSMANTHUS DELAVAYI

This is a valuable addition to the range of really sweet smelling flowers. In late March, occasionally earlier, it will be covered with little ivory-white tubular flowers sticking stoutly out from the rather stiff twigs and very dark green foliage. It is a neat and not very vigorous grower but reasonably hardy and in time should make a shrub six or seven feet in height. It was first raised from seed collected by the Abbé Delavay in Yunnan in 1890, and it is recorded that of the first collecting only one seed germinated.

PARROTIA PERSICA

This shrub is best known for its brilliant autumn colouring, but it also has charming although not very conspicuous flowers in February and March, often being in flower at the same time as *Hamamelis mollis*. Parrotia comes from Persia and the Caucasus and in time will make a small tree. It is very hardy and the flowers seem to be little damaged by frost. Unfortunately, however, they are short lived, since their colour is provided by the reddish anthers which cluster together and cast a reddish glow over the plant, especially when seen from below. The flowers otherwise are not very brilliant and are clustered together in tight little knots at the end of short side branches. Parrotia belongs to the same family as the Hamamelis and also flowers on the bare branches.

PIERIS

The hanging snowy-white tassels of *Pieris japonica* are one of the most delightful sights of an early spring in the wild garden at Wisley. In a favourable season the little white bells will open at the end of February and will hang during March before they finally brown in April. Each is like the little bell of a lily of the valley and as white. They are very freely borne in pendulous racemes four inches in length. There are also several pink forms of which the deepest in colour is 'Daisen', selected from those growing on a mountain of that name in Japan. For cultivation this pieris requires the same treatment as rhododendrons, and some shelter from early morning sun and north-easterly winds will benefit it. It is a slow growing plant at first but in time it will make a large shrub ten feet in height.

Pieris floribunda flowers a few weeks later and the spikes are erect. It is a North American plant from Georgia. The flowers are also bell-like but slightly smaller than those of the previous species and the spikes slightly shorter, but nevertheless it is a desirable plant being a rather more compact grower than the Asiatic species. The flowers are always ranged formally on one side of the stem – the side tending to be the under.

Pieris forrestii is a slightly more delicate plant than either of these and its attraction rests in the brilliant scarlet of the young shoots and leaves. They range from shrimp-pink to a strong scarlet and seem to glow with light in the early spring, often opening in March. They have something of the flamboyance of a tropical poinsettia and at this season there is no more striking plant for the garden. The only trouble lies in the susceptibility of these young leaves to frosts and cold winds. If possible a position with some protection should be chosen, but I have seen this plant grown most successfully both in Surrey and Essex, while it is wonderful at Bodnant in north Wales. Again an acid soil is preferable. There are several varieties and it is important to select a good one in the spring. The flowers are white, the panicles large and they come later in April and May although they overlap the season of the scarlet foliage, and the white flowers and scarlet young growth are delightful together. Later the foliage turns a rather anaemic pale olive green, but about July assumes the real green shade of summer. The finest form is 'Wakehurst'. This plant, although often listed in catalogues as *Pieris forrestii*, is more correctly described as *Pieris formosa* var. *forrestii* and under this name it was given a R.H.S. Award of Garden Merit in 1944.

RIBES

The common flowering currant *Ribes sanguineum* is as popular as it is valuable. It is a plant which will grow equally well both in a shady and a sunny position and a group of the fine red variety 'Splendens' will make a great show of colour from the middle of March till early April, depending on the season. The flowers are borne in short pendulous racemes and appear when the leaves are still small. It is important to choose a good form as some of the pink ones are rather anaemic, and I certainly prefer those like 'Splendens' with as strong a red as possible. Another good deep red form is 'Atrorubens', while 'King Edward VII' and 'Pulborough Scarlet' are clones with deeper colouring. Sprays of any form may be picked and forced in a warm house into flower in February or early March, in which case they are likely to appear somewhat blanched and ghostlike especially if forced in a dark place, and without the leaves they make a striking decoration. All the Ribes look well with a sprinkling of early flowering bulbs at the base such as blue muscari or *Anemone blanda*.

SARCOCOCCAS

A small genus of evergreen, winter-flowering shrubs. The flowers are small and inconspicuous but they are valuable for their scent which is very strong. A few cut twigs will usually scent a warm room, while I well remember driving up one sunny winter's day to the late Mr Lewis Palmer's house near Winchester and being met by a strong blast of such sweet scent that I have never forgotten it. This came from a low two foot hedge of Sarcococca along the front of the house. These shrubs are sometimes called 'Sweet Box' or 'Christmas Box' from the resemblance of the foliage to a box. The flowers are followed by black or dark red berries. The main species grown are *S. confusa* which is very fragrant in flower and will grow up to five or six feet, *S. hookerana* var. *digyna* which has narrower leaves and is less tall, *S. humilis* which is the most dwarf in growth usually not more than two feet, and *S. ruscifolia* var. *chinensis* which flowers a little later usually in mid February to early March and also has red berries.

*   *   *

SCHIZOSTYLIS

These are really autumn-flowering plants but they flower so late in the year that in a mild autumn they will frequently continue from October into November, and there is a beautiful pink variety named after 'Viscountess Byng' which carries the season on into December. Another good pink variety has been named after Mrs Hegarty. The flowers of the type are red and borne up the stem not unlike those of a small gladiolus, and are two inches or more across. The form 'Major' of *S. coccinea* has the largest flowers. *Schizostylis* is a native of South Africa and consequently flowers best after a warm summer in which the fibrous, almost tuberous, rootstocks have been partially baked. It increases very freely from offshoots which spring up all round like blades of grass. It is a good plant for a very warm sunny border under a south wall or for pans in a cool greenhouse. It should never be allowed to become very dry.

STERNBERGIA

These, too, are really autumn-flowering plants but they often run over into the winter months and there are also several true winter-flowering species. The common species is *S. lutea* and this grows freely throughout the Mediterranean, especially on limestone. It has a fair claim to be the biblical 'Lily of the Field'. I have seen it in the south of Italy glowing in yellow masses mingled most attractively with white rocks and pink *Cyclamen neapolitanum*. The flowers are crocus-like, brilliant yellow, and the bulbs flower best in a narrow sunny border at the foot of a wall or greenhouse, where they can get well baked. The variety *angustifolia* seems to flower better in England than the type.

The finest flowering species is *S. clusiana* which used to be known as *S. macrantha* and bears its great golden eggs in late autumn. They are larger than those of *S. lutea* and sit close to the ground almost like a yellow tulip. It seems, however, to be a very shy flowerer in the open and is perhaps best grown in a pan in the alpine house or the bulb frame. The early spring-flowering species is *S. fischeriana* from Kashmir and its brilliant yellow flowers should appear in February or March. It is quite hardy though not so vigorous, but again does best in a warm border where it can be well baked in summer, and the flowers only open on bright sunny days. All the sternbergias take a couple of years to establish themselves and do well on chalk.

SYCOPSIS SINENSIS

A free-flowering evergreen member of the Hamamelis family which bears during February yellow petal-less flowers in clusters. The yellow stamens are tipped with crimson and a large bush, as is the one by the temperate house at Kew, has a quiet attraction and distinction and it will grow and flower against a north wall quite happily.

Berries and Fruits in Winter

There are many coloured berries which will add greatly to the brightness of the winter scene. Different berries are very variable both in the length of time which they will remain on the plant and in their palatability to birds. This latter is a most important factor. The following is only a small selection of plants chosen both for their natural distinction and for their survival qualities. The majority of berried shrubs colour best and produce most fruit in sunny positions and many, such as *Cotoneaster horizontalis*, are seen to best effect against a wall, especially a white wall.

Arbutus menziesii. The Madrona of North America. A large shrub or small tree with attractive cinnamon bark and in the best forms large panicles of orange, red or scarlet berries produced in October and hanging during a fine November. A particularly fine form of this arbutus was given a First Class Certificate by the R.H.S. in the autumn of 1946. It is hardy enough in all except very cold gardens. The flowers are creamy-white with a greenish tinge. Other strawberry trees are described in the chapter on bark and under 'Some Other Good Winter Plants'.

Callicarpa bodinieri var. *giraldii*. This shrub bears during October thick clusters of berries of a most unusual, almost wicked colour – a strong mauve-magenta with more blue than red – and the effect is accentuated by the glossiness of the berries. It presents a most striking effect in indoor decorations. It makes a large shrub in time, five to eight feet in height. The flowers are pale mauve, but not very large. Callicarpas should be planted in groups to ensure effective pollination. They do best in rather sheltered positions. Slightly more tender are *C. dichotoma* and *C. japonica*, both of which have lilac-violet coloured berries, although there is also a rare white form of *C. japonica*. They are not, however, any great improvement over *C. bodinieri* var. *giraldii*, the plant usually grown.

Celastrus orbiculatus, a very vigorous, woody climber, of which the young stems twine over any support. At first the fruit consists of a green three-valved capsule, but when this opens it reveals a most unusual and attractive combination of colours, the seeds being scarlet, while the inside of the capsule is a strong golden-yellow. This beautiful and rampageous climber is often exhibited very well at the R.H.S. autumn Tree and Shrub Competitions. Mr Bean states that the fruits have no attraction for birds and describes it as 'the most striking of all hardy climbers during November, December and January'. Celastrus bear their male and female flowers usually on separate plants and this is frequently the cause of failure to fruit where only one is grown. There is, however, an hermaphrodite form which has flowers of both sexes and one should be careful to order this. Celastrus do not fruit as very young plants so it is particularly important to get the right one from the start or else to plant a group. Their best support is an old tree as they will quickly outgrow most posts.

Clerodendrum trichotomum. This shrub or small tree bears bright turquoise-blue berries backed with deep crimson-purple persistent sepals opening flat or slightly recurved, a most unusual and attractive combination. It is quite hardy and likes an open position and should be much more widely grown than it is. The fruits are preceded by starry white strongly scented flowers in September. The variety *fargesii* is very similar and sometimes fruits more freely. The fruits are a lighter blue but the sepals are not so strongly coloured, so that I prefer the type.

Cotoneasters: a vast clan out of which I would pick the following:

C. conspicuus and its variety *decorus*, a small shrub with neat evergreen foliage and short, stiff branches bearing very large numbers of brilliant scarlet berries. The variety *decorus* has pendulous branches. The berries are very persistent and a large plant of this on the bank by the old greenhouses at Wisley was a fine sight even in February. The berries of this cotoneaster are as brilliant in colour and as persistent as those of any shrub I know. Kingdon-Ward, who discovered it in

(*Above*) *Rhododendron* 'Tessa Roza', a very early flowering hybrid of great beauty. (J. E. Downward)

(*Right*) *Rhododendron* × *praecox*, flowers very early and with great freedom. (Reginald A. Malby & Co.)

(*Above*) *Viburnum* ×
bodnantense 'Deben' has
pure white flowers. (J. E.
Downward)

(*Left*) *Viburnum carlesii*, a
fine specimen. (Reginald
A. Malby & Co.)

Salix aegyptiaca, the earliest willow to flower in January. (J. E. Downward)

Fluffy willow catkins decorate the late winter landscape. (Helmut Gern-sheim)

(*Above*) *Abeliophyllum distichum* has spicy aromatic flowers. (J. E. Downward)

(*Below*) *Arbutus unedo* has strawberry-like fruits and white flowers together. (J. E. Downward)

Bergenia 'Ballawley', whose splendid foliage goes red in winter, also has good reddish purple flower heads. (J. E. Downward)

Chaenomeles japonica, has bright reddish flame coloured flowers in winter or very early spring. (Reginald A. Malby & Co.)

Cornus mas has heads of acrid yellow flowers on leafless branches in February or early March. (J. E. Downward)

Fatsia japonica is distinctive both for its flower and its foliage. (J. E. Down-ward)

Forsythia × *intermedia*
'Spectabilis'. (Reginald
A. Malby & Co.)

Pieris japonica flowers in
February and early
March. (Reginald A.
Malby & Co.)

Garrya elliptica has long suede grey catkins in January and February.
(Reginald A. Malby & Co.)

Ribes sanguineum. (Reginald A. Malby & Co.)

Celastrus orbiculatus, a most spectacular climber with red fruits held against yellow capsules. (J. E. Downward)

south-east Tibet, describes it as a 'bubbling red cauldron of berries'.

C. franchetii var. *sternianus*. A large evergreen shrub with most conspicuous fruits, sealing-wax red in colour, varying to orange-red, borne very abundantly and well displayed against a rather grey-green foliage which is almost white on the under surface of the leaves. This is one of the best cotoneasters. Like the majority of the genus it grows and berries best in an open sunny situation. In a half-shaded place it tends to make a lanky and rather ill-shaped shrub. This used to be widely grown under the name *C. wardii*.

C. frigidus, a large, rather loose-growing shrub or small tree which is covered with deep red berries, which are very persistent, frequently lasting till the New Year.

C. horizontalis is closely allied to *C. conspicuus;* the scarlet berries and foliage are slightly smaller, but the berries are borne with great abundance and it is an excellent shrub for covering banks or walls. In a sunny position the leaves also colour a brilliant scarlet, so that the whole plant seems to glow in the winter sunlight.

'Watereri', both with deep crimson berries very freely produced, and 'Exburyiensis' or 'Rothschildianus' with yellow fruit, but these all require plenty of space.

Crataegus lavallei. This is one of the best of the thorns and frequently the large scarlet fruits hang till February. 'Carrierei' is now regarded as a clone of this hybrid. It is a quick growing plant and in time makes a small tree. The fruits are threequarter inch diameter and the white flowers nearly an inch across. The foliage also colours an attractive bronzy-red in autumn, although it is not as bright as some of the other thorns such as *C. crus-galli* or *C. prunifolia*, another useful fruiting species, but with rather smaller fruits. *Crataegus durobrivensis* is another very fine fruiting species, which is not planted nearly as frequently as its value for winter decoration would indicate. The fruits are scarlet and half an inch in diameter and hang well into the New Year. The fruits of these thorns do not seem to be taken by birds, as some of the other berries are. That curious and legendary plant the Glastonbury Thorn, a form of the common hawthorn, sometimes produces a winter crop of flowers as well as young foliage in addition to flowering at the usual time, and flowers have been recorded on it on Christmas Day. It is exciting to have the hawthorn scent then. The trees are descended by vegetative propagation from an old one at Glastonbury Abbey said to have grown from the staff that Joseph of Arimathea stuck into the ground. Now there is only a young tree at Glastonbury.

Euonymus semiexsertus. September, October and up to mid-November are the months when the majority of the spindle trees give their finest display, but this species retains its fruits much later than the others and is often full of colour during December. It is a deciduous species from Japan and the capsules of the fruit gradually darken during November to a deep rose-pink, revealing the blood-red seed and deep orange and red aril, the fleshy skin covering them. It forms a large bush or small tree and thrives best in an open situation. It is now sometimes regarded as a variety of *E. hamiltonianus*. The fruits are very freely borne and resemble those of the common English spindle, but this species drops its fruits during October. Of the European spindles probably the best is the variety *intermedius* of *E. europaeus*, with peculiarly fine orange-red seeds backed by deep crimson fruits.

Hippophae rhamnoides, the sea-buckthorn, a native plant but still one of the most decorative berried plants available for English gardens. The deep yellow berries are freely borne and combine most harmoniously with the grey-green foliage, which is silvery underneath and generally so arranged that a good deal of the silver is visible. A rather loose-growing shrub, the buckthorn is probably best grown in thickets of several plants together. It is especially successful by the sea, and the fruits are not usually taken by the birds and so hang through the winter. The male and female flowers are borne on separate bushes, so that it is necessary to plant one male bush among a group of female.

Idesia polycarpa. An uncommon tree which bears in October

large pendulous branches of big deep brick-red but matt-surfaced berries, backed by large cordate leaves and pink petioles. It is recorded as being quite hardy at Kew, where it fruits annually. The fruits often remain till December or January. The flowers are yellow-green and inconspicuous. The male and female flowers occur on separate bushes so that it is necessary to plant a group of both sexes.

Ilex aquifolium, the holly, is still one of the very best of our shrubs and trees for winter effect. It is important to secure a good form and if possible it should be allowed to grow freely. Mr W. Robinson recommended transplanting in May and using only seedlings or plants on their own roots not more than three or four feet in height, advice not to be lightly disregarded. However, the various named varieties are more often grafted, but most of them can be propagated successfully from cuttings. Of the red fruited ones I can recommend *I. altaclarensis* 'J.C. van Tol', 'Pyramidalis' and 'Camelliifolia' which have larger leaves than the type, and in the case of 'Camelliifolia' are almost spineless. 'Bacciflava' is a good yellow-fruited holly which usually fruits freely. The variegated leaved hollies are also valuable in winter but they are discussed in the chapter on foliage.

Iris foetidissima, 'the Gladwin or Stinking iris'. The seed heads of this iris are most decorative in winter. The flowers are of no consequence in summer, but in late autumn the spathe withers and the outer seed coat splits to reveal the large bright orange-red seeds which adhere to the outer coat for a long time, so that at Christmas or through January they can be picked and added to any dried decoration or placed in a vase with stylosas. The foliage is evergreen and the plants are quite decorative and build up into large clumps either in full sun or semi-shade and seem to require very little attention throughout the year.

Malus. The crab apples are beautiful both in flower and in fruit: in fact, they are among the best of the small trees for winter fruiting. The two which seem to last longest on the trees, frequently from late autumn into February, are 'Golden

Hornet' and *M.* x *robusta*. 'Golden Hornet' is a wonderful tree and hardly ever seems to fail to fruit. The fruits are quite large, round to oval in shape and a really good deep yellow. They are worth a focal point in the garden where they can be seen from the windows in winter. *M.* x *robusta* has round bright scarlet fruit and can be very decorative. Another crab which retains its fruit well is 'Crittenden', a hybrid with bright scarlet fruit retained through much of the winter. It was raised at Crittenden House in Kent and is now becoming more readily available. Of the other crab apples the older 'John Downie' and 'Dartmouth' are still two of the best for their large decorative fruits which make excellent jelly, but in most seasons they will have fallen by mid-November.

Pernettya. These are ericaceous bushes and should be grown under the same conditions as rhododendrons. The best species is *P. mucronata* and a group of plants of these will quickly form a suckering thicket, usually not much over three feet in height and covered with large fleshy berries about the size of marbles, varying in colour from deep reddish-purple through various shades of purple and pink to white. Most of the forms bear only the one sex in their flowers so that at least one male must be planted in the group. One, however, 'Bell's Seedling' is hermaphrodite with both sexes and dark red berries, but even so it is better to plant a small group rather than a single bush. A good group can also be made out of 'Davis's Hybrids' which have larger berries than the type and vary in colour. The best white is 'White Pearl'.

Physalis franchetti should be planted in a corner of the vegetable garden where it can spread. The colour in this case is derived from an inflated balloon-like calyx which surrounds the seeds and which hangs on the plant like a small Chinese lantern of brightest orange-scarlet. Some call them 'Cape Gooseberries' or 'Winter Cherries'.

Pyracantha. These are useful evergreen shrubs, commonly grown against walls but this is by no means necessary. They produce very large numbers of berries during September and October. Unfortunately these seem to be rather palatable to birds and in a cold season will have all vanished before December. The best are *Pyracantha rogersiana* and *P. atalantioides*, often known justifiably as firethorns, while the *P. coccinea* 'Lalandei' bears more orange and larger fruits than the other two. There is also a good yellow-berrying form of *P. atalantioides*. All pyracanthas are much better grown on their own roots than when grafted on to other stocks. Pyracanthas on a wall should be pruned hard back as soon as the berries have dropped, otherwise it is not possible to keep them to a reasonable shape.

Skimmia japonica. Another attractive evergreen shrub bearing deep red berries about the size of holly berries. These are not, however, taken by the birds and frequently last on the bush throughout the winter. Again male and female flowers are borne on separate bushes and one male plant should be grown to every six females. The best female form is 'Foremanii', and for the male pollinator either 'Fragrans' or 'Rubella' which is also decorative in flower since the buds are red. *S. reevesiana*, which used to be known as *S. fortunei*, has both sexes in the same flowers and can be planted with the *S. japonica* and the fruits sometimes last through the winter until the flowers come in April, but they are not quite so large as those of *S. japonica*. The plants spread freely by suckering and make good ground cover, rarely exceeding three feet in height. If the weather is very bad at flowering time it helps the setting of a good crop of fruit if the flowers are pollinated by hand.

Snowberry. The common snowberry is *Symphoricarpus rivularis* which grows more strongly than *S. albus*. They are both North American and bear from October onwards clusters of large berries, about the size of marbles and glistening white. The branches are slender so that the fruits weigh them down near the ends and dangle like weights on a fishing rod. Apparently they contain something which birds dislike for they are never touched, and so last often throughout the winter. While they will grow almost anywhere either in sun or shade, the size and number of the berries is increased by good cultivation. A range of hybrids with coloured berries has been raised in Holland, and the group has been named *S*. x *doorenbosii* after Dr Doorenbos, a much beloved park superintendent at The Hague. The best of these is probably 'Mother of Pearl', a compact upright grower which makes quite a good loose hedging plant. The berries are smaller, though, than in the other types. *S.* x *chenaultii*, another hybrid, has small purplish-red berries, but I still like the snowy-white ones best.

Sorbus. The common native mountain ash *Sorbus aucuparia* is one of the most rewarding of all trees for late autumn decoration, both for its wonderful autumn colouring and great clusters of orange-scarlet fruits. No one will quickly forget the rowans in Scotland after a good season. There are many other good species whose differentiation is a matter of some difficulty. Among the best are *S. americana* and *S. scalaris* with very large bunches of scarlet fruits, and *S. hupehensis* with glaucous foliage and bunches of pale fruit almost white but mottled with coral-pink. Unfortunately the birds take the berries early so that few of the orange-red fruited ones seem to last long into the winter. The white and pink fruited ones and sometimes even the yellow ones seem to last longer, and I have seen fruits still hanging on *Sorbus hupehensis* after Christmas and long after the leaves have been shed. *S. vilmorinii* has fern-like foliage and clusters of small deep pink berries which also hang late. This species makes usually a smaller and more dense tree and is well worth a place. Among the white fruiting species *S. cash-miriana* is probably the best, the berries being as large as the snowberry. 'Joseph Rock' is rather a mystery plant since its origin is unknown but it has always been associated with that great American plant collector. It may be an undescribed species from China or a naturally occurring hybrid. It is one of the finest species for autumn colour, while the berries are pale yellow and borne in large clusters and often escape early bird damage. I think that this is the sorbus which I would choose first if I should be restricted to a single one.

Symplocos paniculata. An uncommon and most unusual small tree which after a warm season bears masses of small brilliant turquoise-blue berries. Each berry is mottled, shining as if with a glaze, and they are borne in small panicles which are slightly pendulous. Apart from the *Clerodendrum trichotomum*, there is no other shrub or tree commonly grown in England with berries of anything like this brilliant shade. The tree is deciduous and the leaves fall before the berries reach their full blueness, thus accentuating the effect. A single specimen does not usually fruit well on its own so it is desirable to plant a group of three or five to be sure of good results. Unfortunately the berries are very popular with the birds, and in order to keep them long on the bush it is necessary to protect them by netting. Still, they are so spectacular that some people would regard both the grouping and the netting as worth while. I remember some wonderful vases of these shown in the late autumn R.H.S. Tree and Shrub Competition, usually from the Savill Garden of Windsor Great Park. This species was formerly grown under the name of *S. crataegoides* and as such may still be found in catalogues.

Viburnum. There is one absolutely splendid species of viburnum which after a favourable season has its branches weighed down with large clusters of small glistening scarlet berries about the size of red currants. I refer to *V. betulifolium*. Unfortunately the berries are also popular with birds, but I have seen bunches of them still remaining till late in November or early December. To secure the best fruiting it is desirable to plant a group as in the case of the *Symplocos*, and to wait a few years, since young bushes rarely fruit well; but it can be well worth it. *V. henryi* is another good fruiting species, but as the winter advances the bright red berries darken and turn black. *V. lobophyllum* is close to *V. betulifolium* but I have rarely seen it fruiting quite so generously. Our ordinary guelder rose, *V. opulus*, can also be very decorative in early winter. The berries have an attractive translucent shining quality and are bright scarlet or yellow in the form 'Xanthocarpum'. These, of course, are not borne on the Snowball tree, the most decorative in flower, which is rightly called 'Sterile'.

Coloured Bark in the Winter Garden

One of the factors rarely considered in planning the garden is the beauty of bark in some trees and shrubs and how such plants can be used as focal points at the end of grass walks or near the house. Yet the bark is an interest that will be with us throughout the year. It is not really seasonal, although in some maples and birches it does vary slightly at different seasons as the older bark peels off to show the young bark, which is more brilliant in colour. The placing of these trees and shrubs with beautiful bark requires care, so that they stand out on their own where the sun shines on them and lights them up against a dark background, if the bark is white or scarlet. Those with mahogany bark are best where they have an open light background or one of green grass. Good bark is complementary also to good form and foliage in the garden, although unfortunately there seem to be very few plants which combine these characteristics. Perhaps the arbutus come nearest to it. We have quite a selection to choose from, arbutus, birches, cherries, dogwoods, maples, rubus and willows, so it seems best to discuss them in order.

Acer (Maples). One of the finest of all trees for its peeling bark is *Acer griseum*, the paper bark maple. The old bark peels off in large flakes to reveal the young bark below which is a bright cinnamon-mahogany. The whole effect is of a rather shaggy warm reddish-mahogany trunk. Young trees should be pruned early so that they develop a tall stem free of side branches. I have seen some with very tall straight trunks drawn up by the surrounding bushes but they do not usually show to best effect in such a situation. The autumn colour of the foliage is also good, a strong reddish-orange, enhancing the bark.

Another first-rate small tree or large bush for winter colour is *Acer palmatum* 'Senkaki', the coral bark maple. The young twigs are a beautiful coral-scarlet, very bright in effect when the

Cotoneaster conspicuus var. *decorus*, one of the brightest red late autumn fruiting shrubs. Sometimes the berries last throughout the winter. (J. E. Downward)

Acer griseum shows its peeling mahogany bark. (H. Smith)

Arbutus × *andrachnoides* has a lovely pinkish mahogany trunk. (H. Smith)

Betula jacquemontii, one of the finest white trunked birches, comes from Kashmir. (H. Smith)

Rubus cockburnianus which used to be called *R. giraldianus*, has white washed stems throughout the winter. (H. Smith)

Picea brewerana, a superb tree for its dark weeping foliage. (J. E. Downward)

sun shines on them in front of a dark background. The effect is only developed in early autumn but lasts throughout the winter. It is unique among the maples and a bush that I would hate to omit from any good garden, where there is space. Even quite young plants are effective. The snake bark maples, particularly *A. grosseri* var. *hersii* and *A. pensylvanicum*, are unusual trees. In these the bark is a yellow-green with wavy longitudinal silvery stripes running up and down the trunk. These are particularly noticeable in young trees, and again a clean trunk should be developed. Others in the same group are *A. capillipes*, *A davidii* and *A. rufinerve* and these are all desirable where there is space, although their garden effect is not very different. If there is only room for one, probably *A. grosseri* var. *hersii* is the best. There is also a red-twigged form of *A. pensylvanicum* called 'Erythrocladum'. I have occasionally seen magnificent plants of this but they are rare and it is often of rather weak constitution. Great care must be taken of the graft when young. I have lost two through damage to the graft in its young stages. All of these have good autumn colour also in the foliage in varying shades between butter-yellow and orange-crimson. They make excellent small trees for the smaller modern garden.

Arbutus (Strawberry Trees). These have already been discussed for their winter-flowering and their fruits, but even more distinctive and valuable are the colour of their bark and their curving and twisting way of growth; it is always a delight to look up into the branches of an old strawberry tree outlined against the sky and for these features the common *Arbutus unedo* is pre-eminent. For bark the hybrid *Arbutus* x. *andrachnoides* is among the best, the trunk varying in shades of silvery-pink and cinnamon-red and peeling to reveal fresh tones melting into each other. Once they have seen them few will forget the venerable specimens of this tree on one of the upper terraces at Bodnant. In the western American Madrono tree, *Arbutus menziesii*, the bark adds to its reddish-mahogany an ochreous tinge which makes a young tree very striking in its native forests and also in the garden. In all cases one wants to be able to approach the trunk and even help in peeling off the old bark, so they should be planted near a walk and not surrounded by other bushes since the colour goes right down to the base.

Betula (Birches). These have some of the finest trees for coloured bark of any genus, both in the creamy or silvery-whites and in the orange-mahogany range, and when well grown make most striking effects. Intending planters should, however, be warned that the full bark colour is not developed in very young trees, but gradually spreads from the base upwards. As in arbutus and *Acer griseum*, the colour can be helped by a little judicious peeling or rubbing off of the old bark when it seems ready to come. Our own native silver birch *B. pendula* is very variable in the colour of its trunks but it is usually a beautiful and graceful tree, sometimes with a fine silvery-white trunk; even more strikingly silver is *B. papyrifera* the paper birch of North America. This in time makes a big tree up to sixty feet and it is surprising that it is not grown more freely. The bark peels off in thin paper-like layers, leaving a smooth stem beneath. These two are quite different in the quality of their whites from those with creamy-white stems which may often have a slightly pinkish undertone. The best of these are *B. jacquemontii* and *B. utilis*, the Himalayan birch. The two are closely related and have some of the most striking bark in the genus. In this connection white is a colour. It is usually better to plant a specimen standing forward near the beginning of a glade since if planted as a focal point at the end, as indeed is often done, it tends to make the glade seem shorter since the eye is immediately attracted to it. This doesn't apply to the mahogany stemmed species. Both the species mentioned, however, are variable and trees of *B. utilis* have been found with light mahogany-brown bark rather than the creamy-white that is much the more desirable. The bark seems to get darker as the origin goes eastwards towards China. Another species with rather similar characteristics is *B. ermanii* which usually has a beautiful pinkish-white trunk merging into darker mahogany colouring in the branches. *B. platyphylla* var. *szechuanica* can also be very beautiful with a conspicuous creamy-white bark. For planting there is probably not much to choose between these Asiatic birches, but it is important to get a good form. Occasionally one sees large trees of them, but more often they make small but graceful trees.

Among those with pinkish or orange-mahogany stems the best is probably *B. albo-sinensis* var. *septentrionalis* and a mature specimen of this with a clear trunk is one of the most beautiful of trees. The trunk is covered with a silvery-grey bloom, and the tones underneath of pink, orange and mahogany seem to melt into each other.

Cornus (Dogwood). The dogwood for winter colour is *C. alba*, named for the colour of its berries. It is a strong grower making thickets of bright crimson stems, especially where it has been cut back and there are plenty of young twigs. The finest form is 'Sibirica', sometimes known as 'Westonbirt'. In this the twigs are a brilliant sealing-wax scarlet growing up to four feet from a pollarded base. It is not so vigorous as the ordinary form but the colour is so much better that it is certainly the one to choose; several clumps of it should be planted to form a group and there will be no brighter colour in the garden all the winter. Once established, it should be cut down nearly to the base in spring. With it may be grown *C. stolonifera* 'Flavi-ramea' which has bright ochreous-yellow stems and should be treated in spring in the same way. Groups of the two contrasting colours are very striking. Such a planting may be seen at Wisley beside the round pond. Both these cornuses are unsuitable for dry places and do well by the edge of a pond or where the soil remains moist.

Prunus serrula. This cherry usually makes a small tree but it has perhaps the finest shining dark reddish-mahogany of all barks. It is like a finely polished piece of old furniture, and an old trunk kept peeled and rubbed over occasionally with a duster is a very fine sight. It must be planted where the sun will light up the trunk. This tree used to be known as *P. serrula tibetica* but apparently there is no other variety and so the third name is not required. It has inconspicuous flowers but some enterprising nurserymen have top grafted more interesting flowering cherries, such as *P. sargentii*, on young specimens so that one can have the advantage of both bark and flower, an ingenious idea but the results are still uncommon and rather expensive.

Rubus cockburnianus. This is a bramble of great vigour in which the dark purplish stems are covered with a silvery-white bloom which makes a thicket of them a very conspicuous sight in winter. It is not, however, a plant for the small garden, but looks well at the edge of an open woodland or in the wild garden where it can be placed against a dark background. This plant is more often found in older books and catalogues under the name *Rubus giraldianus*. It should be cut back hard in spring so that it makes plenty of young growth, a prickly job. The flower and fruit are not particularly decorative but the foliage is fernlike with a number of leaflets which are white or silvery-grey beneath.

Willows (Salix). There are several willows with very decorative bark. The brightest are forms of *S. alba*. The scarlet-twigged willow is *S. alba* 'Chermesina', often known as 'Britzensis'. A pollarded group of these can make a very brilliant winter spectacle. I well remember one such near the entrance to the Savill Gardens in Windsor Great Park, standing up like flaming fires out of the snow. They will grow into quite big trees but to get the most brilliant scarlet effect from the young twigs they are best kept to a short trunk and cut back hard each spring. The yellow-twigged *vitellina*, the Golden Willow, is also very conspicuous. In late February or early March the yellow twigs and freshening green growth of the best of the weeping willows, *S.* x *chrysocoma*, is a sight to which we always look forward and one which heralds the beginning of the change from winter to spring. It is a hybrid between *S. alba* and the ordinary weeping willow *S. babylonica*. Willows with a white mealy bloom on their young stems are also decorative in winter and the best of these is *S. irrorata*, which also has good catkins. A group of these contrasted with 'Chermesina' can be very effective and such a planting has been made in the winter garden of the Cambridge Botanic Garden. *S. daphnoides* also has an attractive white bloom on its bark in winter and also has large furry catkins. The willows are so easily propagated from cuttings, or even from large slips taken in autumn and plunged in the open ground, that they should be planted much more freely for their colour in winter.

Form and Foliage in the Winter Garden

In the winter the importance of evergreens with interesting form or foliage becomes particularly apparent, and one tends to look more at the plant architecture and the trees of the garden than at its individual flowers. Green is such an interesting colour and has such infinite variations that it can make the garden seem furnished, while a garden of only deciduous trees and herbaceous plants can be dull in the winter months. The contrast made by a tall columnar tree or, even better, a group of them, with one that has branches spreading horizontally is nearly always successful. A splendid example of this is the group at Westonbirt Arboretum of *Libocedrus* (*Calocedrus*) *decurrens*, tall narrow columnar conifers of dark green, with *Parrotia persica* which is deciduous but has splendid autumn colour. Westonbirt is so full of good examples of contrasted planting that it is well worth a visit at any time, as much in winter as in summer. There are several good contrasting groups there also of spreading blue-green cedars or cypresses with upright conifers beside them, some yellow-green and some darker green. The brightness of some of the yellow foliaged upright cypresses such as 'Winston Churchill' or 'Stewartii', or even the Golden Yew, helps to light up the garden in winter when the sun shines, and makes a focal point in a way that the dark greens and blue-greens do not, splendid as they are in summer when the shadow makes them seem even darker.

Among the Lawson cypresses there is great variety. Two of the best narrow bluish columns are 'Grayswood Pillar' and 'Columnaris' and these do not spread nearly as widely as the older 'Allumii' or 'Triomphe de Boskoop'. The Italian cypress is superb for a narrow columnar green tree in the milder areas; for the colder areas 'Kilmacurragh' rivals it and gives the garden a Mediterranean look. One of the best of the slow growing blue cypresses is 'Pembury Blue' and it takes a long time to make a large tree. *Cupressus glabra* 'Pyramidalis', under which name the tree usually grown as *C. arizonica* 'Glauca' should now be known, is also a good feature in any garden, however small, and in this country rarely seems to grow too large. They have fine feathery foliage and look well planted in a small group. For those who are patient an arch of yew like the one leading to the pond at Hidcote is a splendid architectural feature, so are yew hedges and they make the best background for other trees.

Those with patience should also plant *Picea brewerana*, surely one of the loveliest and most graceful of all conifers with its drooping green branchlets and needles silvery below. All connoisseurs seem always to stop and admire and photograph in front of it. But as a young plant it is terribly slow to grow, only a few inches a year, while it does not form its weeping habit until it is ten or more years old. But it is worth waiting for. It is one of the few trees which look even better after rain when the drooping branchlets are covered with silvery drops, gradually dripping down like sparkling necklaces. There are good examples both at Sheffield Park and at Westonbirt. If one cannot easily obtain *Picea brewerana*, or if one is not prepared to wait for its maturity, *Picea omorika* 'Pendula' is a very lovely tree which grows much more quickly and has the same slender upright form with drooping branchlets which shine with silver in the wind from the glaucous underneath of the needles.

For the milder areas the conifer which always gives me the greatest pleasure is the glaucous form of *Pinus montezumae* from Mexico, but unfortunately young plants of it are very rare. The needles are very long, six inches or more, and silvery-blue, and the whole effect is unique among trees. The finest specimens are at Mount Usher in Ireland, a garden open regularly to the public, but there are very good trees of it also at Sheffield Park in Sussex, a National Trust garden, and at Grayswood Hill in Surrey which also is often open, while at the Bicton Arboretum in Devonshire there is a lovely young tree standing by itself on a lawn.

For the smaller garden the dwarf conifers give tremendous

variety in form and colour and make good features. One should not underestimate, however, the eventual height of some of them when planted out. I have seen some sold as dwarf conifers now twenty feet tall. Others, however, are true dwarfs and there is plenty of information now available about their eventual sizes in Hillier's invaluable manual as well as in specialist books on dwarf conifers. Most have rather cumbersome names but there are no other ones to use for them. For a very regular and compact bright green pyramid, *Picea glauca albertiana* 'Conica' is deservedly one of the most popular. Hillier reckons that it will take thirty years to grow to six feet. Among the dwarf golden conifers with rather flat upright branches *Chamaecyparis lawsoniana* 'Minima Aurea' or 'Aurea Densa' are both distinct and suitable for any position, while rather larger but equally golden is *Chamaecyparis obtusa* 'Crippsii' which has more horizontal feathery growth, while a complete contrast is the horizontal spreading *Picea pungens* 'Procumbens' which has very striking stiff glaucous-blue branches spreading over the ground. These make a good variety of colour intermingled with heathers, while for a narrow columnar glaucous spire the well known Irish juniper, *Juniperus communis* 'Hibernica', is still unrivalled and some fine old specimens can be seen in the heather garden at Wisley which, incidentally, is as good to visit all through the winter as in summer. For a smothering green spreading mass to cloak a man-hole cover or some other feature where one cannot plant directly, the forms of *Juniperus horizontalis* are excellent. The bluest are 'Blue Harbor' and 'Glauca', while 'Plumosa' is one of the best feathery greens.

Other solid masses of dark green, which can be trimmed to make architectural features, are provided by the bays and the hollies such as 'Pyramidalis' and 'Camelliifolia' and these make splendid backgrounds for the hamamelis or the viburnums or the white daphnes. The variegated hollies are also well worth growing and brighten up any corner. On a recent visit to the big collection of hollies in Hillier's arboretum near Romsey I picked out 'Handsworth New Silver', 'Golden Queen' and 'Golden King', the latter female, the former male! It is

The grey needled form
of *Pinus montezumae* from
Mexico.

(*Above*) *Jasminum polyanthum* will make a cool greenhouse in winter smell like a scent shop. (H. Smith)

(*Below*) *Rhododendron* 'White Wings', another good scented rhododendron for the cool greenhouse. (J. E. Downward)

unfortunate that now the names cannot be swopped over. 'Silver Queen' is another good variety, again a misnamed male. It has silvery-white margins to the leaf. There are many other strongly variegated plants and in general I find them rather a disrupting element in the garden, but in the winter they can be valuable and I do like the very golden variegated elaeagnus such as *E. pungens* 'Dicksonii' or 'Maculata', the former having the golden colour more on the edges of the leaves, the latter splashed on it in irregular blotches. The variegated Euonymus, mostly forms of *E. japonicus*, are strong elements in the garden making dwarf compact pillars tipped and margined with yellow or cream, while the more spreading forms of the variegated *E. fortunei* and *E. radicans* are among the most eye-catching in colour of all variegated plants and require careful placing.

Rhododendrons should also be considered as valuable foliage plants and are almost infinite in their variety. The finest blue foliaged one for the large rock garden is *R. lepidostylum* which makes low mounds for the peat garden or the large rock garden, decorative all the winter. There are superb specimens in the Edinburgh Botanic Garden over six feet across and four feet tall, but this size is very unusual and a low mound two or three feet across and a foot and a half high is much more usual. The leaves are small and the whole makes a dense compact shrub, which should be grown for its foliage alone since its pale creamy-yellow flowers are small and inconspicuous. It is really blue. Many of the large-leaved rhododendrons make magnificent plants for gardens in the milder areas, but it is no use planting them in hot, dry or very windy places. They are primarily plants for the open woodland garden. Some of the leaves may be two foot or more long and nearly a foot across, thick, leathery and glossy in *R. sinogrande* and *R. macabeanum*, the latter having a polished silvery-grey underside to the leaf. *R. falconeri* is no less distinctive with a greenish matt leaf above and rusty brown indumentum beneath. These make trees in time but will remain under ten feet in height for many years. It is only in frost when the leaves droop and curl up that these rhododendrons look really miserable but they soon recover as the ground thaws. Smaller in leaf are *R. bureavii*, *R. fulvum* and *R. arboreum* 'Sir Charles Lemon', all of which have thick rusty brown indumentum on the underside of the leaf which shows up strongly as the wind moves the leaves.

Camellia foliage is also valuable in the winter for its shiny polished look, quite irrespective of its flower. Probably the numerous forms of *C. japonica* and *C.* x *williamsii* are the best for this: then they become dual-purpose shrubs. The growth is usually thicker and more compact where the plants get some sun.

Eucalyptus are light and feathery and glaucous in many species and are as decorative in winter as in summer. They should not be cut back till the coldest of the winter is over. I particularly like the juvenile foliage of some of the glaucous ones such as *E. coccifera*, *E. niphophila*, *E. perriniana* and *E. urnigera* 'Glauca'. If cut back in spring one can retain them as fairly compact bushes, which for smaller gardens are preferable to the large trees which they can become in the milder areas.

For fine foliage one need not be restricted to shrubs, some of the herbaceous plants such as the bergenias make splendid ground cover, and the large, shiny, shield-like leaves turn from their rich glossy green to a burnished coppery-crimson. The best one for this is 'Bellawley' where the leaves are often a foot across and remain all through the winter. The leaves curve gently rather than lying flat and the plants spread quite freely. For this evergreenness they are superior as plants to the hostas which die away completely in winter. They last well also when cut. Another good foliage plant which we find invaluable both for its place in the garden and for cutting for a bowl with stylosa irises is the variegated arum *A. marmoratum pictum*, and many visitors crave bits of this. Luckily it increases freely but the tubers go deep and need a large fork to dig them up. The scarlet seed heads, larger than those of our native 'Lords and Ladies', also last well into the early winter. Equally valuable as marbled ground cover is the foliage of *Cyclamen neapolitanum* and one can grow snowdrops through it. The variegated ivies are also great decorators for the garden at this time: the large leaved yellow-blotched *Hedera canariensis* 'Variegata' for the warmer areas, or the smaller and more dainty silver and green leaved 'Glacier' or the more yellow 'Gold Heart'. We should make much more use of them as they propagate and spread so easily. Some are even edged with rosy-red in winter, such as 'Tricolor'. Most of these colour best if grown in a fairly dry sunny position but they can also be grown in semi-shade. Another plant that we find very decorative through the colder months is the golden variegated periwinkle and we have a row of this under a lonicera hedge. If the long streamers are cut back it will encourage the younger shoots to grow erect and there make a brightly coloured mass about a foot or two tall. We also use it for covering old stumps which are difficult to get out.

The green flowered hellebores, such as *H. corsicus* and *H. foetidus*, make splendid greenery all the winter, while the horned poppies *Glaucium corniculatum* have a very striking glaucous silvery-blue rosette that lasts well through the cold season. It is one of our best plants for winter effect in a sunny place. Another splendid plant for foliage effect is the New Zealand flax *Phormium tenax* which throws up great stiff blue-grey broadsword-like leaves four or five feet tall. It grows best in a damp position. In an old clump the ten foot seed heads of rusty brown also last through the winter. For cutting, the old seed heads of grasses are unsurpassed and when dry will last for months. They can be enlivened with the orange-red lanterns of *Physalis* and other dried flowers. For a hot, dry position the Moroccan daisy *Leucanthemum hosmariense* makes a splendid silvery-grey mound and the large daisies open frequently all through the winter. It is excellent planted in a dry wall.

The mass of good foliage plants is so great that here we have only mentioned a few of my favourites. I hope it will encourage gardeners to be more adventurous in their planting for winter effect as well as summer colour.

The Cool Greenhouse in Winter

This is the time when we enjoy most the cool greenhouse, in January when it can be full of camellias with finer and more perfect blooms than one is likely to find in the open, particularly among the large doubles. Under these conditions some of the tender rhododendrons and the mimosas will come into flower while the abutilons seem to flower incessantly. The old-fashioned winter conservatory was full of flowering bulbs and forced pot plants such as the Persian cyclamen, schizanthus and tender primulas, for instance *P. malacoides* and *P. obconica*, and very colourful the result was. These certainly last in flower best in the cool greenhouse but to get them into flower in January and February or even earlier requires more heat and much labour. Much more labour-saving is the cool greenhouse planted out with shrubs such as the superb one in the Savill Garden of Windsor Great Park or even the temperate house at Kew. The larger the better, but still much can be done in a far smaller house, say twenty-five by fifteen feet, and only a very little heat need be given so that the frost is just kept out. We set our thermostat at 36° or 38°F. and it is sufficient, although more heat up to 45°F. would bring on some of the flowers earlier, but would use double the amount of electricity. I find such a house also more restful and interesting than the Edwardian type of winter conservatory.

Our earliest winter colour usually comes from that superb royal purple *Tibouchina semidecandra*, now sometimes and perhaps more correctly called *T. urvilliana;* it usually starts to flower in late September or early October and continues right through till January, after which it should be cut back to the lowest pair of shoots at the base of the new wood. The flowers are the strongest purple of any flower I know and each is several inches across, opening nearly flat as a saucer with stamens and stigmas sticking out like a many-pronged pitch-

The Cool Greenhouse in Winter

fork. The leaves are rich green and velvety. Although it comes
from southern Brazil it has been grown out of doors against a
warm wall in a warm part of Cornwall, but for most gardens it
must be regarded as a greenhouse plant. It is easily propagated
from cuttings of the prunings and will flower as quite a small
pot plant. Planted out in the greenhouse it will quickly reach the
roof, growing three to four feet in a season if not regularly
pruned.

Before Christmas the first camellia will be out. This is
usually *C. sasanqua* 'Narumi-gata' which has quite large creamy-
white flowers, flushed with pink towards the edges, and this
seems to flower much better in England under glass than in the
open. In warmer climates it does not need this protection. This
is quickly followed by some of the forms of *C. japonica* although
the time of opening does vary appreciably from season to
season. One of the earliest for us is usually 'Daitarin', more
often known in England as 'Hatsu-zakura'. It has large single
pale pink flowers with a big mass of stamens and petaloids
in the centre. It is well worth growing a plant inside for
this early-flowering habit. Otherwise we grow chiefly inside
the larger flowered semi-doubles and full doubles. The
two largest of all, both from America, are 'Drama Girl', with
bright crimson-red semi-double flowers like soup plates rather
than saucers, sometimes up to eight inches across; and 'Mrs
D. W. Davis', with semi-double pale blush-pink flowers of
nearly the same size. It is very beautiful but so large and
heavy are the flowers that they are inclined to droop unless a
firm framework of strong branches is built up by pruning
when the plant is young. A lovely salmon-pink double is
'Faith' and each year this gives us more flower than any other.
In autumn we usually disbud the plants, leaving only a single
bud on each short shoot. Thus one obtains finer flowers.
Another delightful salmon-pink double is 'C.M. Wilson', an
American sport with paler flowers from the old 'Elegans' which
can also be very beautiful in a cool house. The semi-double
white camellias such as 'Gauntlettii' and 'Haku-rakuten' also
open their flowers to perfection in such a house which they

seldom do outside, and they are so lovely. Recently raised are several charming varieties from New Zealand and these have looser semi-double flowers than some of those I have just mentioned. I particularly like 'Anticipation' which has *C. saluenensis* as one parent but still has flowers four to five inches across of rather bright crimson; also the paler salmon-pink 'Grand Jury' which has 'Salutation' as one parent and was also raised by Mr Jury. The flowers are semi-double with wavy petals and a large almost paeony-form centre. These are both rather tall slender growers.

If one has space, as in the greenhouse at the Savill Gardens, few plants can be more magnificent than the old camellia 'Captain Rawes', semi-double form of *C. reticulata*, but if left unpruned it will in time reach twenty or more feet. Still, one can enjoy a smaller plant for many years before one has to raise the roof and it will stand some pruning back. The flowers are immense, often six inches across, with wavy petals of glowing rich crimson. It is probably still unsurpassed by the more recently introduced varieties from Kunming although these are magnificent: I like particularly the semi-double very pale pink 'Buddha' and the larger 'Crimson Robe'. A single variety with bright crimson flowers which seems to make a more compact lower bush and always flowers early, generally for Christmas, under glass for us is 'Mary Williams', a selected seedling from the single form of *C. reticulata* introduced by George Forrest long after the semi-double one.

There are innumerable varieties to choose from. If I had a larger house I would like to plant also some I have seen recently in other collections, but would not now want to turn out any I have for them. I have particularly noted and liked the following among the varieties of *C. japonica*: 'Betty Sheffield Supreme', with white double flowers, each petal being edged with deep pink as in a Picotee carnation; 'Tomorrow Park Hill', a large pink semi-double, slightly variegated; 'Barbara Woodruff', another sport from 'Elegans', and 'Edelweiss', a very beautiful single or semi-double creamy-white with a good boss of yellow stamens in the centre.

The rhododendrons which benefit so much from a little winter protection are members of the *Maddenii* series and some of these, such as *R. lindleyi*, have lily-like trumpet-shaped flowers of the purest waxy white, four or five inches long so that even if they were hardier they would still benefit from the glass. In my opinion there is no rhododendron flower more beautiful than a truss of three or four of these great flowers, which are also delicately scented. In order to make a more bushy shrub out of a natural straggly grower the non-flowering buds should be removed before they start to grow so that the shoot may branch out as if it had flowered. Nearly as fine is *R. dalhousiae* which has slightly more tubular flowers, usually tinted creamy-yellow or even pale lemon-green, but it is seldom such a good grower. *R. veitchianum* with slightly smaller deeply cleft white flowers tinged with green at the base, *R. ciliicalyx* with white flowers often suffused with pale rose and *R. cubittii* which has both white and pink forms, usually with a conspicuous orange-brown blotch at the base, are all excellent for such a house and will give a good reward in February and March. So will some of the hybrids of this group. I find 'White Wings' the most rewarding and my plant never fails to be covered with large white scented flowers early each spring. These are slightly larger and have slightly more substance than the flowers of the older 'Lady Alice Fitzwilliam' and 'Fragrantissimum' which also make such splendid tub plants for bringing into the house. Their long shoots can be tied down or pruned so that the whole makes a fairly compact dome of flower, and they are strongly scented. For the very large house *R. nuttallii* and its hybrid 'Tyermannii' have even larger flowers but it is difficult to keep them to bushy shrubs and they tend to reach eight or more feet quickly. The dwarf *R. leucaspis* can also be enhanced in flower by the protection of such a house and will there flower in February. As a plant it is hardy enough to grow outside in most areas, but so often the flowers get damaged or frosted, spoiling their pure creamy-white beauty. The same applies to some of its hybrids such as 'Bric-à-Brac' but this seems with us to get damaged outside less frequently, as does *R.*

moupinense. All these can, however, be grown inside and will flower well.

Both the rhododendrons and the camellias appreciate a soil mulched with leaf mould and peat and no lime and plenty of water when they are making their new growth.

From Australia and New Zealand the *Epacris* flower from late autumn through the early part of the winter and do not require more heat than the rhododendrons mentioned. The leaves are small and narrow like heathers and the flowers are borne freely along the branches. In colour they vary from white through pink to deep red. Those grown are mostly forms of *E. impressa* but there are a number of other species. They require similar conditions to the camellias and rhododendrons and mingle well with them. They should certainly be more widely grown than they are. So should the Cape heaths, but unfortunately they are not good mixers with other plants and do best in a house on their own. However, *Erica canaliculata* will in most houses cover itself with its little white bells speckled with the dark brown anthers from February till April. They require plenty of ventilation at all times when it is not frosty outside.

I find the *Prostantheras* also good greenhouse plants for February and March flowering, in particular *P. ovalifolia*, and they are very little trouble and can be kept reasonably compact as long as they are cut back hard after flowering. They make twiggy bushes up to four or five feet and are covered with purplish-mauve flowers like little snapdragons. Young plants are easily propagated from cuttings.

Some climbers may also be admitted to such a house. *Lapageria*, both in its crimson and its white forms, can be very lovely with its large waxy bells dripping from the wall in early winter. *Jasminum polyanthum* has about the finest scent of any cool greenhouse plant but it is a very rampant grower and will quickly cover a wall. For this reason some gardeners prefer to restrict it to a tub but it seldom does so well under such conditions. The long sprays of pink-budded white flowers are delightful but unfortunately they do not last well when cut for the house. For the large greenhouse or old conservatory a couple of tree ferns, *Dicksonia antarctica*, or one of the *Cyatheas* will be very lovely and can be kept in growth all the winter. Their arching is so graceful and they give the appearance of tropical luxuriance without requiring the temperature of a tropical house, but they do take a good deal of space; when full grown they have a span of eight foot or more. If one were willing to keep a minimum temperature of 45°F. one could also grow *Cymbidium* orchids satisfactorily with them, although not completely in their shade.

A house which is planted out on lime soil is more difficult. One could, however, do much with raised peat beds there and dwarf rhododendrons. Alternatively one could accept the limy soil and plant it instead with bulbs interspersed with the small shrubby *Lithospermum rosmarinifolium* whose gentian-blue flowers will decorate it for much of the winter. *Daphne odora* should also grow well and flower early and help to scent the house, as will also *Jasminum polyanthum*.

The abutilons are also good in either soil. The three coloured little bells of *Abutilon megapotamicum*, red, yellow and purple, seem to be produced summer and winter under such conditions while the larger-flowered hybrids such as 'Ashford Red' or 'Nabob', deep crimson and heavily veined, and the bright lemon-yellow 'Golden Ball' or 'Golden Fleece', slightly more open in its bell, grow quickly into large bushes covered with flowers, or may be trained up on a single stem and then allowed to spread over the roof dripping their flowers. They must be cut hard back at intervals. The same applies to the mimosas when grown under glass and these will quickly become too large for any except the large house but there they will be very lovely. Under such conditions I prefer the blue-grey leaved *A. baileyana* or *A. podalyrifolia* which has even larger clusters of flowers. Under glass they need cutting back after flowering. 'Exeter hybrid' is another excellent one for growing in the larger greenhouse. It has more flexible growth and so is easier to train along the roof and I have seen some wonderful plants of this like a ceiling of gold in February or early March.

In general the range of suitable plants for such a house is so great – and I have only been able to mention a small proportion of them – that I can only recommend you to visit the great botanic gardens such as Kew and Edinburgh, Oxford and Cambridge and also Wisley, in winter as well as summer, and browse awhile in their temperate houses. From the beginning of March also the Savill Garden in Windsor Great Park is generally open to the public, and its temperate house is very well worth a visit.

Index

Index

Abeliophyllum distichum, 111; Ill.
  btwn pp. 128/9
Abutilons, 153
  A. 'Ashford Red', 153
  A. 'Golden Ball', 153
  A. 'Golden Fleece', 153
  A. megapotamicum, 153
  A. 'Nabob', 153
Acacias, 111–12
  A. armata, 112
  A. baileyana, 112, 153
  A. dealbata, 18, 111–12
  A. 'Exeter hybrid', 153
  A. podalyrifolia, 153
Acers, 136–8
  A. capillipes, 137
  A. davidii, 137
  A. griseum, 12, 136, 138;
    Ill. btwn. pp. 136/7
  A. grosseri var. *hersii*, 137
  A. palmatum 'Senkaki', 136–7
  A. pensylvanicum, 137
  A. p. 'Erythrocladum', 137
  A. rufinerve, 137
Aconites, 31, 50–1
Adonis, 112–13
  A. aestivalis, 112
  A. amurensis, 112–13
  A. vernalis, 112
  A. wolgensis, 113
Almonds, 22, 79–80, 82
Alnus, 113
  A. cordata, 113
  A. glutinosa, 'Imperialis', 113
  A. g. 'Laciniata', 113
  A. incana 'Aurea', 113
  A. i. 'Laciniata' 113
  A. i. 'Ramulis Coccineis', 113
Amaryllis belladonna, 12
Anemones, 24–7, 53, 59, 64
  A. appenina, 25
  A. blanda, 24–6, 124;, Ill.

facing p. 32
  A. b. atrocoerulea, 24; Ill. facing p.
    32
  A. b. 'Charmer', 24
  A. b. ingrami see '*atrocoerulea*'
  A. b. 'Radar', 24
  A. b. var. *scythinica*, 25
  A. b. 'Violetta', 24
  A. b. 'White Beauty', 24–5
  A. coronaria, 25–6
  A. c. de Caen strain, 25
  A. c. Giant French strain, 25
  A. c. 'His Excellency' see
    'Hollandia'
  A. c. 'Hollandia', 25
  A. c. 'Lord Lieutenant', 25
  A. c. 'Mr Fokker', 25
  A. c. St Brigid strain, 25–6
  A. c. 'Sylphide', 25
  A. c. 'The Admiral', 25
  A. c. 'The Bride', 25
  A. c. 'The Governor', 25
  A. fulgens, 25–6
  A. hepatica, see under Hepatica
  A. nemorosa, 26
  A. n. 'Allenii', 26; Ill. facing p.
    32
  A. n. 'Royal Blue', 26
  A. n. 'Vestal', 26
  A. pavonina, 26
  A. St Bavo strain, 25–6
Apricots, 82
Arbutus, 114, 136, 137–8
  A. andrachne, 114
  A. x. andrachnoides, 114, 137;
    Ill. btwn pp. 136/7
  A. menziesii, 114, 127, 137
  A. unedo, 114, 137; Ill. btwn pp.
    128/9
  A. u. '*Rubra*', 114
Arum marmoratum pictum, 146

Bergenias, 114–15, 146
  B. purpurascens 'Ballawley', 114,
    146; Ill. btwn pp. 128/9
Betula albo-sinensis var.
  septentrionalis, 138
  B. ermanii, 138
  B. jacquemontii, 138; Ill. btwn
    pp. 136/7
  B. papyrifera, 138
  B. pendula, 138
  B. platyphylla var. *szechuanica*, 138
Birches, 136, 138–9
  silver, 12

Callicarpas, 127
  C. bodinieri var. *giraldii*, 127
  C. dichotoma, 127
  C. japonica, 127
Calluna vulgaris, 89–90
  C. v. 'Alportii', 89
  C. v. 'Blazeaway', 90
  C. v. 'Else Purnell', 89
  C. v. 'Gold Haze', 90
  C. v. 'Golden Feather', 90
  C. v. 'Hammondii', 89
  C. v. 'H. E. Beale', 89
  C. v. 'J. H. Hamilton', 89
  C. v. 'Peter Sparkes', 89
  C. v. 'Serlei', 89
Camellias, 21–2, 73–7, 81, 146,
  148–9
  C. 'Cornish Snow', 75
  C. cuspidata, 75
  C. japonica, 73–6, 146, 149
  C. j. 'Adolphe Audusson', 76
  C. j. 'Alba Simplex', 77
  C. j. 'Anticipation', 150
  C. j. 'Barbara Woodruff', 150
  C. j. 'Betty Sheffield Supreme',
    150
  C. j. 'C. M. Wilson', 149
  C. j. 'Daitarin', 149
  C. j. 'Devonia', 77
  C. j. 'Drama Girl', 149
  C. j. 'Edelweiss', 150
  C. j. 'Elegans', 149–50
  C. j. 'Faith', 149

C. j. 'Gauntlettii', 149–50
C. j. 'Grand Jury', 150
C. j. 'Haku-rakuten', 149–50
C. j. 'Haku-zakura' *see* 'Daitarin'
C. j. 'Jupiter', 77
C. j. 'Lady Clare', 76
C. j. 'Magnoliaeflora', 76–7
C. j. 'Mrs D. W. Davis', 149
C. j. 'Nobilissima', 77
C. j. 'Peach Blossom', 77
C. j. 'Salutation', 150
C. j. 'Tomorrow Park Hill', 150
C. j. 'White Swan', 77
C. reticulata, 21, 73, 75–7, 150
C. r. 'Buddha', 150
C. r. 'Captain Rawes', 150
C. r. 'Crimson Robe', 150
C. r. 'Mary Williams', 150
C. r. 'Noble Pearl', Ill. btwn pp.
  48/9
C. saluenensis, 74–5, 150
C. sasanqua, 73
C. s. 'Briar Rose', 74
C. s. 'Hiryu', 74
C. s. 'Narumi-gata', 74, 149
C. x williamsii, 74–5, 146
C. x w. 'Anticipation', 74
C. x w. 'Donation', 74; Colour
  pl. facing p. 97
C. x w. 'Grand Jury', 74
C. x w. 'J. C. Williams', 74
C. x w. 'Mary Christian', 74
C. x w. 'November Pink', 74
Celandines, 59
Celastrus orbiculatus, 128; Ill.
  facing p. 129
Chaenomeles, 115–16
  C. cathayensis, 115
  C. japonica, 115; Ill. btwn pp.
    128/9
  C. speciosa, 115
  C. s. 'Cardinalis', 115
  C. s. 'Moerloosii', 115
  C. s. 'Nivalis', 115
  C. s. 'Phylis Moore', 115
  C. superba, 115
  C. s. 'Knaphill Scarlet', 115
  C. s. 'Rowallane', 115

Chamaecyparis lawsoniana 'Allumii',
142
C. l. 'Aurea Densa', 144
C. l. 'Columnaris', 142
C. l. 'Grayswood Pillar', 142
C. l. 'Kilmacurragh', 142
C. l. 'Minima Aurea', 144
C. l. 'Pembury Blue', 142–3
C. l. 'Stewartii', 142
C. l. 'Triomphe de Boskoop', 142
C. l. 'Winston Churchill', 142
C. obtusa 'Crippsii', 144
Cherries, flowering, 78–9
Cherries, Japanese, 83, 87
Chimonanthus praecox, 14, 116
C. p. 'Grandiflorus', 116
C. p. 'Luteus', 116
Chionodoxas, 51, 53–4, 82
C. gigantea, 54
C. luciliae, 53–4; Ill. facing p. 41
C. sardensis, 53–4
C. siehei, 53–4
Chionoscillas, 53
C. allenii, 53
C. a. 'Fra Angelico', 53
Clematis, 116–17
C. cirrhosa, 116–17
C. c. var. balearica, 117
Clerodendrum trichotomum, 128, 135
C. t. var fargesii, 128
Colchicum ancyrense, 55
C. bifolium, 55
C. brachyphyllum, 55
C. kesselringii, 55
C. variegatum, 55
Conifers, 142–4
Cornus alba, 117, 139
C. a. 'Sibirica', 139; Colour pl.
facing p. 97
C. a. 'Westonbirt' *see* 'Sibirica'
C. chinensis, 117
C. mas, 117; Ill. btwn pp. 128/9
C. sanguinea, 117
C. stolonifera 'Flaviramea', 139;
Colour pl. facing p. 97
Corylopsis, 117–18
C. pauciflora, 118
C. platypetala, 118

C. sinensis, 118
C. spicata, 118
C. veitchiana, 118
Cotoneasters, 128–9
C. conspicuus, 99, 128–9; Ill.
btwn 136/7
C. c. decorus, 128; Ill. btwn 136/7
C. 'Exburyiensis', 129
C. franchetii var. sternianus, 129
C. frigidus, 129
C. horizontalis, 127, 129
C. 'Rothschildianus', 129
C. wardii see franchetii var.
sternianus
C. 'Watereri', 129
Crataegus, 129
C. 'Carrierei', 129
C. crus-galli, 129
C. durobrivensis, 129
C. lavallei, 129
C. prunifolia, 129
Crocuses, 19, 28–33; Ill. facing p.
40
C. aerius, 31
C. aureus, 55
C. balansae, 30
C. biflorus, 30
C. b. var. weldenii, 31
C. boryi, 29
C. chrysanthus, 17, 23, 31–2
C. c. 'Blue Pearl', 31
C. c. 'Cream Beauty', 31
C. c. 'E. A. Bowles', 31; Ill.
facing p. 33
C. c. 'Gipsy Girl', 31
C. c. 'Goldilocks', 31
C. c. 'Ladykiller', 31
C. c. 'Saturnus', 31
C. c. 'Snow Bunting', 31
C. c. 'Sultan', 32
C. c. 'Warley White', 32
C. c. 'Zwanenburg Bronze', 32
C. dalmaticus, 30
C. imperati, 29
C. korolkowii, 30
C. kotschyanus, 29
C. laevigatus, 29
C. l. var. fontenayi, 29

C. medius, 29
C. niveus, 29
C. nudiflorus, 29
C. olivieri, 17, 30
C. sieberi, 32
C. s. 'Bowles's White', 32
C. s. heterochromos see *s. versicolor*
C. s. tricolor, 32
C. s. versicolor, 32
C. s. Attic Variety, 32
C. s. 'Violet Queen', 32
C. speciosus, 29
C. s. 'Cassiope', 29
C. s. 'Oxonian', 29
C. susianus (Cloth of Gold), 17, 30
C. tomasinianus, 30; Ill. btwn pp. 40/1
C. t. 'Barr's Purple', 30
C. t. 'Taplow Ruby', 30
C. t. 'Whitewell Purple', 30
C. tournefortii, 29
C. vernus, 30
C. v. 'Jeanne d'Arc', 33
C. v. 'Kathleen Parlow', 33
C. v. 'Negro Boy', 33
C. v. 'Purpureus Grandiflorus', 33
C. v. 'Vanguard', 33
C. zonatus see *kotschyanus*
Cupressus arizonica 'Glauca', 143
C. cashmeriana, 81
C. glabra 'Pyramidalis', 143
Cyatheas, 153
Cyclamen, 31, 33–6, 148
C. africanum, 34
C. atkinsii, 34
C. balearicum, 35
C. cilicium, 34
C. coum, 34–5, 52; Colour pl. facing p. 96
C. creticum, 35
C. cyprium, 34
C. europaeum, 33–4
C. graecum, 34
C. hederifolium see *neapolitanum*
C. hiemale, 34
C. ibericum, 34

C. libanoticum, 35–6
C. neapolitanum, 33–4, 106, 125, 146
C. orbiculatum, 34
C. persicum, 35–6
C. pseudibericum, 35
C. purpurascens see *europaeum*
C. repandum, 35–6
C. vernum, 34
Cydonia oblonga, 115
Cymbidiums, 153
Cypresses, 12, 142–3

Daffodils, dwarf, 19, 39–44
Daphnes, 17, 64, 84–6, 144
D. blagayana, 85; Ill. btwn pp. 48/9
D. laureola, 86
D. mezereum, 14, 84–5; Ill. btwn pp. 48/9
D. m. 'Bowles's White', 84
D. odora, 86, 153
D. o. 'Aureomarginata', 86
D. pontica, 86
Dicksonia antarctica, 153
Dogswoods, 136, 139

Edgeworthia papyrifera, 86
Elaeagnus pungens 'Dicksonii', 145
E. p. 'Maculata', 145
Epacris, 22, 152
E. impressa, 152
Eranthis cilicica, 51
E. hyemalis, 51; Ill. facing p. 41
E. pinnatifida, 51
E. x. tubergenii, 51; Colour pl. facing p. 96
E. t. 'Guinea Gold', 51
Erica arborea alpina, 89, 91
E. australis, 91
E. a. 'Mr Robert', 91
E. canaliculata, 152
E. carnea, 85, 90; Ill. btwn pp. 48/9
E. c. 'King George', 90
E. c. 'Springwood Pink', 90
E. c. 'Springwood White', 90
E. c. 'Vivellii', 90

E. c. 'Winter Beauty', 90
E. codonodes, 91
E. darleyensis, 90
E. lusitanica, 91
E. mediterranea, 90
Erythroniums, 56–8
E. californicum, 57
E. critinium, Ill. facing p. 48
E. dens-canis, 56–7
E. hendersonii, 57
E. 'Kondo', 57
E. oregonum, 57
E. 'Pagoda', 57
E. 'Pink Beauty', 57
E. revolutum, 57
E. r. var. *johnsonii*, 57
E. tuolumnense, 57
E. 'White Beauty', 57; Colour
pl. facing p. 96
Eucalyptus, 146
E. coccifera, 146
E. niphophila, 146
E. perriniana, 146
E. urnigera 'Glauca', 146
Euonymus europaeus intermedius, 130
E. fortunei, 145
E. hamiltonianus, 130
E. japonicus, 145
E. radicans, 145
E. semiexsertus, 130

Fatshedera lizei, 119
Fatsia japonica, 118–19; Ill. btwn
pp. 128/9
Forsythias, 22, 119
F. giraldiana, 119
F. x. intermedia, 119
F. x i. 'Beatrix Farrand', 119
F. x i. 'Lynwood', 119
F. x i. 'Spectabilis', Ill. btwn pp.
128/9
F. ovata, 119
F. 'Spectabilis', 119
F. suspensa, 119
F. s. atrocaulis, 119
Fritillaries, 56, 58
F. acmopetala, 58; Ill. facing p.
48

F. crassifolia, 58
F. meleagris, 58

Galanthus byzantinus, 45
G. corcyrensis, 45
G. elwesii, 45
G. graecus, 45
G. nivalis, 44
G. n. 'Atkinsii', 45
G. n. 'John Gray', 45
G. n. 'Magnet', 45
G. n. 'Sam Arnott', 45
G. n. 'Straffan', 45; Ill. btwn
pp. 40/1
G. plicatus, 45
G. p. 'Warham', 45
G. reginae-olgae, 44–6
Garrya elliptica, 120; Ill. btwn pp.
128/9
Glaucium corniculatum, 147
Grape hyacinths, 54, 82

Hamamelis, 18, 64, 85–8, 144
H. japonica, 87–8
H. j. arborea, 87
H. j. zuccariniana, 87
H. 'Jelena', 88
H. mollis, 18, 87–8, 100, 122;
Ill. facing p. 49
H. m. 'Brevipetala', 88
H. m. 'Coombe Wood', 88
H. m. 'Goldcrest', 88
H. m. 'Pallida', 87–8; Colour pl.
facing p. 80
H. 'Ruby Glow', 88
H. vernalis, 88
H. virginiana, 88
Heathers, 89–92
Heaths, Cape, 22, 152
Hebes, 120–1
H. 'Autumn Glory', 120
H. 'Midsummer Beauty', 120
H. speciosa 'Evelyn', 120
H. s. 'Gauntletti', 120
H. s. 'La Seduisante', 120
H. s. 'Simon Delaux', 120
Hedera canariensis, 147
H. c. 'Variegata', 147

H. 'Glacier', 147
H. 'Gold Heart', 147
H. 'Tricolor', 147
Hellebores, 11, 19, 61–4, 147
Helleborus argutifolius, 62
H. atrorubens, 63; Ill. btwn pp.
48/9
H. colchicus, 63
H. corsicus, 62, 64, 147
H. foetidus, 64
H. guttatus, 63
H. lividus, 62
H. niger, 61; Ill. btwn pp. 48/9
H. n. 'Altifolius', 61
H. n. 'Macranthus', 61
H. n. 'Potter's Wheel', 61
H. n. praecox, 61
H. x nigricors, 62
H. orientalis, 63
H. o. 'Black Knight', 63
H. x sternii, 62
H. viridis, 64
Hepaticas, 53, 59–60
H. angulosa, 60
H. 'Ballardii', 60
H. nobilis, 60
H. transsilvanica, 60
H. triloba, 60
Hippophae rhamnoides, 130
Hyacinthus amethystinus, 55
H. azureus, 55
H. orientalis, 55

Idesia polycarpa, 130–1
Ilex, 131
I. altaclarensis 'J. C. van Tol', 131
I. aquifolium, 131
I. a. 'Bacciflava' 131,
I. a. 'Camelliifolia', 131, 144
I. a. 'Golden King', 144–5
I. a. 'Golden Queen', 144–5
I. a. 'Handsworth New Silver',
144
I. a. 'Pyramidalis', 131, 144
I. a. 'Silver Queen', 145
Ipomoea bona-nox, 21
Irises, 36–9, 131
I. alata see *planifolia*

I. aucheri, 38
I. bakeriana, 38
I. caucasica, 39
I. danfordiae, 16, 37–8
I. foetidissima, 131
I. histrio, 37
I. h. aintabensis, 37
I. histrioides, 16, 36–8
I. h. major, 37–8; Ill. facing p.
40
I. 'Katharine Hodgkin', 37
I. nicolai, 39
I. persica, 38–9
I. planifolia, 39
I. reticulata, 16, 31, 37–9
I. r. 'Blue Veil', 38
I. r. 'Cantab', 38
I. r. 'Clairette', 38
I. r. 'Harmony', 38
I. r. 'Hercules', 38
I. r. 'Jeanine', 39
I. r. 'Joyce', 39
I. r. 'J. S. Dijt', 38
I. r. 'Royal Blue', 39
I. r. 'Spring Time', 39
I. r. 'Violet Beauty', 39
I. r. 'Wentworth', 39
I. sindjarensis see *aucheri*
I. 'Sindpers', 38
I. stylosa see *unguicularis*
I. unguicularis, 11–12, 14–16, 36,
39; Colour pl. facing p. 80
I. u. var. *cretensis*, 15
I. u. 'Ellis's Var', 15
I. u. var. *lazica*, 15
I. u. 'Marginata', 15
I. u. 'Mary Barnard', 15; Ill.
facing p. 16
I. u. 'Walter Butt', 15
Irises, dwarf, 31, 38

Jasmine, 85
Jasminum mesnyi, 14
J. nudiflorum, 11–14; Ill. facing
p. 16
J. polyanthum, 152–3; Ill. facing
p. 145
J. primulinum, 14

Juniperus communis, 91–2 'Hibernica', 144
  J. horizontalis 'Blue Harbor', 144
  J. h. 'Glauca', 144
  J. h. 'Plumosa', 144

Lapageria, 152
Leucanthemum hosmariense, 147
Leucojum aestivum, 47
  L. vernum, 46; Ill. btwn pp. 40/1
  L. v. var. *carpathicum*, 47
  L. v. var. *vagneri*, 47
Libocedrus decurrens, 142
Lithospermums, 68–70
  L. diffusum 'Heavenly Blue', 69
  L. rosmarinifolium, 69–70, 153
Lonicera, 121, 147
  L. fragrantissima, 121
  L. x purpusii, 121
  L. standishii, 121
Lysichitum americanum, 66

Magnolias, 92–7
  M. campbellii, 92–7; Colour pl. facing p. 81
  M. c. 'Charles Raffill', 95
  M. c. 'Kew's Surprise', 96
  M. c. 'Lanarth', 95
  M. c. subsp. *mollicomata*, Ill. facing p. 65
  M. dawsoniana, 95–6
  M. denudata, 92, 95, 97
  M. kobus, 93
  M. 'Leonard Messel', 93
  M. x loebneri 'Merrill', 93
  M. mollicomata, 95–6
  M. salicifolia, 93
  M. sargentiana, 92, 95–6
  M. s. var. *robusta*, 96
  M. x soulangiana, 97; Ill. facing p. 64
  M. sprengeri var. *diva*, 96
  M. stellata, 97; Ill. facing p. 65
  M. s. rosea, 92–3
  M. veitchii, 95–7
Mahonias, 98–100
  M. acanthifolia, 100
  M. aquifolium, 98, 100

M. bealei, 99
M. 'Buckland', 100
M. 'Charity', 99; Ill. facing p. 112
M. 'Hope', 100
M. japonica, 98–100
M. lomariifolia, 99
M. napaulensis, 100
M. pinnata, 100
M. 'Undulata', 100
Malus, 131–2
  M. 'Crittenden', 132
  M. 'Dartmouth', 132
  M. 'Golden Hornet', 131–2
  M. 'John Downie', 132
  M. x robusta, 132
Maples, 136–8
Mimosa, 111–12, 148
Muscaris, 54, 124
  M. armeniacum 'Heavenly Blue', 54
  M. botryoides, 54
  M. latifolium, 54
  M. neglectum, 54
  M. paradoxum, 54
  M. racemosum, 54

Narcissus asturiensis, 42; Ill. btwn pp. 40/1
N. 'Bartley', 43
N. 'Beryl', 20
N. bulbocodium, 40, 42, 54
N. b. var. *citrinus*, 41
N. b. var. *conspicuus*, 41
N. b. var. *obesus*, 41
N. b. var. *romieuxii*, 40
N. cantabricus, 40
N. c. var. *petunioides*, 40; Ill. btwn pp. 40/1
N. 'Charity May', 43
N. clusii, 40
N. 'Cragford', 44
N. cyclamineus, 20, 41–3
N. 'Dove Wings', 43
N. elegans, 40
N. eystettensis, 42
N. foliosus, 40
N. 'Golden Harvest', 44

N. 'Grande Monarque', 44
N. 'Jack Snipe', 43
N. 'Jana', 43
N. 'Jenny', 43
N. 'Minicycla', 42
N. minimus, 42
N. minor, 42
N. monophyllus, 40
N. 'Muslin', 40
N. 'Nylon', 40
N. obvallaris, 42
N. 'Peeping Tom', 43
N. pseudonarcissus, 42
N. p. 'W. P. Milner', 20
N. pumilus, 42
N. 'Rembrandt', 44
N. 'Scilly Isles White', 44
N. serotinus, 40
N. 'Soleil d'Or', 44
N. 'Tarlatan', 40
N. triandrus, 42–3, 54
N. t. var. *albus*, 43
N. t. 'February Gold', 43
N. t. var. *loiseleurii*, 43
N. viridiflorus, 40
N. watieri, 43–4
Nerine bowdenii, 12

Osmanthus delavayi, 121–2

Parrotia persica, 122, 142
Peaches, 22, 80–2
Pelargoniums, 22
    P. 'Paul Crampel', 22
Periwinkles, 60, 147
Pernettyas, 132
    P. mucronata, 132
    P. m. 'Bell's Seedling', 132
    P. m. 'Davis's Hybrids', 132
    P. m. 'White Pearl', 132
Phormium tenax, 147
Physalis franchetii, 132, 147
Picea brewerana, 143; Ill. facing p.
    137
    P. glauca albertiana 'Conica', 144
    P. omorika 'Pendula', 143
    P. pungens 'Procumbens', 144

Pieris, 122–3
    P. floribunda, 123
    P. forrestii, 123
    P. f. 'Wakehurst', 123
    P. formosa var. *forrestii* see
      forrestii
    P. japonica, 122; Ill. btwn pp.
      128/9
    P. j. 'Daisen', 122–3
Pinus montezumae, 143; Ill. facing p.
    144
Plums, 82–3
Populus euphratica, 110
Primulas, 64–8, 148
    P. allionii, 67–8
    P. 'Barrowby Gem', 67
    P. bhutanica see *whitei*
    P. clarkei, 66; Ill. btwn pp. 48/9
    P. edgeworthii, 64–6; Ill. btwn pp.
      48/9
    P. 'Galligaskins', 67
    P. 'Jack-a-napes', 67
    P. 'Madame de Pompadour', 67
    P. malacoides, 148
    P. obconica, 148
    P. 'Pantaloons', 67
    P. rosea, 66
    P. r. 'Delight', 66
    P. scapigera, 66
    P. sonchifolia, 66
    P. 'Wanda', 19, 23, 67;
      Ill. btwn pp. 48/9
    P. whitei, 66; Colour pl. facing
      p. 97
    P. winteri see *edgeworthii*
Prostantheras, 152
    P. ovalifolia, 152
Prunus, 77–83
    P. x amygdalo-persica 'Pollardii',
      79–80; Ill. btwn pp. 48/9
    P. x blireana, 83; Ill. btwn pp.
      48/9
    P. campanulata, 79
    P. cerasifera, 83
    P. conradinae, 78
    P. c. semi-plena, 78–9
    P. davidiana, 80–1
    P. 'Fudan Zakura', 83

P. incisa, 79
P. i. 'February Pink', 79
P. i. 'Praecox', 79
P. 'Kursar', 79
P. mume, 82
P. m. 'Beni-shi-don', 82
P. 'Okame', 79
P. persica 'Aurora', 82
P. p. 'Iceberg', 82
P. p. 'Russell's Red', 82
P. pissardii, 82-3
P. sargentii, 79, 140
P. serrula, 12, 139-40
P. s. tibetica see *serrula*
P. serrulata, 12
P. s. 'Amano-gawa', 79
P. s. 'Kanzan', 79
P. subhirtella var. *autumnalis*, 78-9
P. s. a. 'Rosea', 78; Ill. btwn
   pp. 48/9
P. s. 'Fukubana', 78
P. pendula 'Rosea', 78
P. tenella 'Fire Hill', 80
P. t. 'Gessleriana', 80
P. triloba, 81-2; Ill. btwn pp.
   48/9
P. yedoensis, 83
Pulmonarias, 68-9
   P. angustifolia azurea, 68
   P. a. 'Mawson's Blue', 68
   P. rubra, 69
   P. 'White Wings', 69
Puschkinia scilloides, 52, 54-5
Pulsatillas, 27-8
   P. alpina, 27
   P. apiifolia, 27
   P. grandis, 27
   P. halleri 'Budapest', 27
   P. sulphurea, 27
   P. vernalis, 27-8; Ill. facing p. 33
   P. vulgaris, 27-8
Pyracanthas, 132-3
   P. atalantioides, 133
   P. coccinea 'Lalandei', 133
   P. rogersiana, 133

Ranunculus asiaticus, 36
   R. ficaria 'Grandiflorus', 59

R. f. 'Major', 59
Rhododendrons, 18-19, 21-2, 73,
   100-5, 145-6, 148, 151-3
R. arboreum, 103-4
R. a. 'Sir Charles Lemon', 146
R. barbatum, 104-5
R. 'Barclayi', 104
R. 'Bo-Peep', 102-3
R. 'Bric-a-Brac', 102, 151
R. bureavii, 146
R. caucasicum, 103
R. 'Chink', 103
R. 'Christmas Cheer', 103
R. ciliatum, 101-2
R. ciliicalyx, 151
R. 'Cilpinense', 102
R. cubittii, 151
R. dalhousiae, 151
R. dauricum, 101
R. eclecteum, 105
R. edgeworthii, 22
R. falconeri, 108, 145
R. 'Fragrantissimum', 151
R. fulvum, 146
R. 'Helen Fox', 104
R. 'Jacksoni', 103
R. keiskei, 103
R. 'Lady Alice Fitzwilliam', 151
R. lepidostylum, 145
R. leucaspis, 18, 101-2, 151
R. lindleyi, 151
R. l. 'Dame Edith Sitwell',
   Ill. facing p. 16
R. lutescens, 102-3
R. l. 'Bagshot Sands', 102
R. l. 'Exbury', 102
R. macabeanum, 145
R. maddenii, 22, 151
R. moupinense, 18, 101-3, 152
R. mucronulatum, 18, 23, 100-1
R. 'Nobleanum', 103
R. nuttallii, 151
R. oreodoxa, 105
R. x praecox, 101, 103; Ill.
   facing p. 128
R. 'Red Admiral', 104
R. 'Robert Fox', 104
R. 'Seta', 103; Ill. facing p. 113

R. 'Shilsoni', 104
R. sinogrande, 145
R. spinuliferum, 103
R. stewartianum, 105
R. sutchuenense, 104
R. s. var. *geraldii*, 104–5
R. 'Tessa Roza', 103; Ill. facing p. 128
R. thomsonii, 104
R. trichocladum, 103
R. 'Tyermannii', 151
R. veitchianum, 151
R. 'White Wings', 151; Ill. facing p. 145
Ribes, 123–4
R. sanguineum, 123–4; Ill. btwn pp. 128/9
R. s. 'Atrorubens', 124
R. s. 'King Edward VII', 124
R. s. 'Pulborough Scarlet', 124
R. s. 'Splendens', 124
Rubus, 136, 140
R. cockburnianus, 140; Ill. btwn pp. 136/7
R. giraldianus see *cockburnianus*

Salix aegyptiaca, 108; Ill. btwn pp. 128/9
S. alba 'Chermesina', 110, 140
S. a. vitellina, 140
S. a. vitellina pendula, 109–10
S. babylonica, 140
S. b. ramulis aureis see *vittelina pendula*
S. caprea, 109
S. c. 'Aglaia', 109
S. x *chrysocoma*, 140
S. daphnoides, 108–9, 140–1
S. fargesii, 110
S. gracilistyla, 109
S. irrorata, 110, 140
S. medemii see *aegyptiaca*
S. melanostachys, 109
S. vitellina britzensis see *alba* 'Chermesina'
Sarcococcas, 124
S. confusa, 124
S. hookerana var. *digyna*, 124

S. humilis, 124
S. ruscifolia var. *chinensis*, 124
Saxifrages, 70–2
Saxifraga apiculata, 72
S. aretioides, 71
S. 'Boydii', 71
S. burseriana, 71
S. 'Faldonside', 71; Ill. btwn pp. 48/9
S. b. 'Gloria', 71
S. b. 'His Majesty', 71
S. b. 'Sulphurea', 71
S. b. 'Valerie Finnis', 71
S. fortunei, 72
S. grisebachii, 71
S. g. 'Wisley Variety', 71
S. 'Irvingii', 71
S. 'Kellereri', 71
S. oppositifolia, 72
S. o. 'Splendens', Ill. btwn pp. 48/9
S. o. 'Wetterhorn', 72
S. retusa, 72
Saxifrages, Kabschia, 20, 70
Schizanthus, 148
Schizostylis, 125
S. coccinea, 12
S. c. 'Major', 125
S. c. 'Mrs Hegarty', 125
S. c. 'Viscountess Byng', 125
Scillas, 51–5
S. bifolia, 52–3; Ill. facing p. 41
S. b. praecox, 52
S. b. taurica, 52
S. sibirica, 52
S. s. atrocoerulea, 52
S. 'Spring Beauty' see *sibirica atrocoerulea*
S. tubergeniana, 52, 55
Skimmias, 133
S. fortunei see *reevesiana*
S. japonica, 133; Colour pl. facing p. 97
S. j. 'Foremanii', 133
S. j. 'Fragrans', 133
S. reevesiana, 133
S. 'Rubella', 133
Snowberry, 133–4

Snowdrops, 19, 31, 44–6, 64,
146; Colour pl. facing p. 96
Snowflakes, 31, 46–7
Sorbus, 134
  S. americana, 134
  S. aucuparia, 134
  S. cashmiriana, 134
  S. hupehensis, 134
  S. 'Joseph Rock', 134
  S. scalaris, 134
  S. vilmorinii, 134
Sternbergias, 125–6
  S. clusiana, 125
  S. fischeriana, 126
  S. lutea, 125
  S. l. var. *angustifolia*, 125
  S. macrantha see *clusiana*
Sycopsis sinensis, 126
Symphoricarpus albus, 133
  S. x chenaultii, 134
  S. x doorenbosii, 133–4
  S. d. 'Mother of Pearl', 134
  S. rivularis, 133
Symplocos crataegoides see *paniculata*
  S. paniculata, 134–5

Tecophilaea cyanocrocus, 56; Ill.
facing p. 48
Tibouchinas, 21–3
  T. semidecandra, 21, 148–9;
Ill. facing p. 16
  T. urvilliana see *semidecandra*
Tulips, 47–50
  Tulipa biflora, 50
  T. fosteriana, 48
  T. greigii, 48
  T. humilis, 47
  T. kaufmanniana, 47, 49; Ill.
btwn pp. 40/1
  T. k. 'Alfred Cortot', 49
  T. k. 'Brilliant', 49
  T. k. 'César Franck', 49
  T. k. 'Fritz Kreisler', 49
  T. k. 'Scarlet Elegance', 49
  T. k. 'Shakespeare', 49

T. k. 'Stresa', 49
T. k. 'The First', 48
T. praecox, 50
T. primulina, 50
T. pulchella, 47
T. saxatilis, 49–50
T. turkestanica, 50
T. violacea, 47–8

Viburnums, 105–8, 135, 144
  V. 'Anne Russell', 107
  V. betulifolium, 135
  V. x bodnantense, 106–7
  V. x b. 'Dawn', 107
  V. x b. 'Deben', 107; Ill. btwn
128/9
  V. burkwoodii, 107
  V. carlesii, 107; Ill. btwn pp.
128/9
  V. farreri, 14, 18, 105–7
  V. foetens, 107
  V. fragrans see *farreri*
  V. grandiflorum, 106
  V. henryi, 135
  V. lobophyllum, 135
  V. opulus, 135
  V. o. 'Sterile', 135
  V. o. 'Xanthocarpum', 135
  V. 'Park Farm Hybrid', 107
  V. rhytidophyllum, 108
  V. tinus, 108
  V. t. 'Eve Price', 108
  V. t. 'French White', 108
  V. t. lucidum, 108
  V. utile, 107
Vinca difformis, 60
  V. major, 60
  V. minor, 60
Violets, 60–1
  Viola 'Duchesse de Parme', 61
  V. 'Princess of Wales', 61
  V. septentrionalis, 61; Ill. btwn
pp. 48/9

Willows, 108–10, 136, 140–1